CHRISTIANITY AND SOCIAL JUSTICE

RELIGIONS IN CONFLICT

JON HARRIS

FORWARD BY RUSSELL FULLER

REFORMATION ZION PUBLISHING

Christianity and Social Justice: Religions in Conflict
© 2021 Jon Harris
Published by Reformation Zion Publishing
Ann Arbor, Michigan
www.reformationzion.com

Published 2021
Printed in the United States of America
ISBN: 978-1-956521-00-9

To my grandparents and the country they love

CONTENTS

FOREWORD

AFTER THE FALL of the Berlin Wall and the collapse of the Soviet Union, the gag line was that Marxism was dead in Europe and the West, except in Cambridge, Massachusetts. The jest, of course, was not directed just at Harvard or all universities, but at the broader culture of America: its newspapers, theaters, televisions, local schools, and to be sure, its universities. In short, it was directed at all the social institutions. Marxism may have died in Eastern Europe and the former Soviet Union a generation ago, but it was nevertheless alive and well in American culture. In fact, today it holds the high ground throughout America, as the front cover of Newsweek magazine declared in 2009: "We are all socialists now."

Downwind from the culture are the political institutions. Political leaders are constantly trying to read where the culture is and where it is going. After all, one step out of the spirit of the age could cost someone their congressional seat and the perks that come with it. They do not move the culture; the culture moves them. Truth be told, our leaders are followers.

In the same way, the visible church is also downwind from culture. The current philosophies and cultural ideas are often gratefully received in the often-compromised visible church. And many church leaders are busy themselves with trying to understand where culture is going. After all, one step out of sync with the spirit of the age could harm the reputation of a pastor, a church, or a ministry. It might even bring reproach, condemnation, and persecution. We do not move the culture; the culture moves us. Our church leaders are often followers of the culture as well.

Progressivism became the dominant political and social position among American elites in the early twentieth century. A large portion of the visible church, keeping up with the times, moved left with the culture to create a gospel in step with the times: the Social Gospel. As the Social Gospel mirrored the political and liberal trends of a hundred years ago, so the Social Justice Gospel of today (or the Woke Gospel) mirrors the political and liberal trends today. Now that a more aggressive form of cultural Marxism is now in vogue with political and secular elites, it is also fashionable in churches and denominations. False gospels always march side by side with the fashions of an increasingly worldly secular culture. This was true a hundred years ago, and it will be true a hundred years from now. False gospels always follow the world. The Woke Gospel advocates are of the world, and the world hears them.

This book is important for genuine Christians because Christians need to understand that the Woke Gospel is not an add-on to the Gospel. It is a replacement of the true gospel. It is another gospel that God's people need to anathematize. Jon Harris masterfully demonstrates with primary sources and careful analysis the dangers of this false gospel. He chronicles the history of Social Justice from the French Revolution to modern times in both secular and "Christian" thought. The solution that Social Justice offers is socialism. Harris shows that Marxism, with a heavy dose of radical racist, feminist, homosexual theories, and postmodernism became the dominate cultural theory of today. As the old Marxists turned Marxism into a secular religion with Stalin and Mao, so the new Marxists have created their new secular religion. This has worked itself into the church as Liberation Theology a generation ago and the Woke Gospel of today. The Woke Church leaders at first made it an add-on to the Christian faith, and then they made the Christian faith an add-on to the Woke Gospel.

Harris then demonstrates how the church has been infiltrated by the Woke Gospel. He uses Scripture to show that the Woke faith is contrary to the Christian faith. The Woke often muddy issues by using terms such as "gospel issue" or "gospel above all" or other biblical sounding terms. They often challenge Christians to accept a "more holistic gospel," something more than just Christ and Him crucified. Instead, they direct us to a whole gospel that can work inside and outside of the church walls and that can "redeem" all society.

Most importantly, Harris names the names of the leaders of this woke religion within evangelicalism. Most books on this issue speak in broad terms about the ideas and philosophies but rarely give names and specifics. Many who write or speak against this false gospel fail to name their own pastors and colleagues who teach and promote this false gospel. They are, in fact, covering for them. Jon Harris calling out by name the leaders of this false gospel, his careful documentation, and his excellent analysis make this the best book on the topic.

Jon Harris concludes that this woke gospel is a different gospel with its confusion of law and gospel; having different ethics of sin, justice, and righteousness; a different epistemology with its standpoint theory, and a different metaphysic based on humanism.

Reading this book brought back many memories of my teaching at Southern Seminary. In particularly, it brought back a meeting in which Al Mohler defended Critical Race Theory and its teachings at Southern Seminary by now Provost, Matthew Hall. Mohler defended the concepts of systemic racism, whiteness, and white privilege, the crown jewels of Critical Race Theory. He concluded his defense of Matthew Hall and Critical Race Theory with a statement that I will never forget: "Marxism has insights."

Jon Harris conclusively demonstrates that these "Marxist insights," the foundation of the Woke Faith, is another gospel contrary to the true gospel of Jesus Christ.

Russell Fuller,
July 2021

INTRODUCTION

IT FEELS LIKE it was yesterday—standing across from my seminary professor in his office as he sat at his desk and motioned for me to close the door. I quickly did so and hurried back, sitting on the edge of the chair facing him and waiting to hear the answer to my important question. He then spoke in something approximating a whisper as if KGB officers could possibly come in at any moment and disrupt our unauthorized meeting. He turned away from his computer, looked me directly in the eye, and warned: "If I were to say what I think about what's going on at this campus I would be fired." My heart sank as I processed the momentary shocking sensation. "How can this be possible?" I thought to myself. This man is both professional and, I assumed, well respected. But it was.

Admittedly, at the time I suspected there was an unspoken rule at Southeastern Baptist Theological Seminary that students, staff, and faculty were not supposed to question or even acknowledge the incursions made by the social justice movement at the school. Almost overnight some of us felt like we were swimming in a sea of political rhetoric, but everyone else acted like it was normal and nothing was happening. I remember sitting in a car with a student friend one warm Southern night struggling to explain the change we both noticed. "It seems an awful lot like Marxism," I observed. "Except, instead of feeling guilty for wealth we are made to feel guilty for being white or conservative."

In some ways, I was probably thinking back to my undergraduate experiences at a secular college. One of my sociology professors openly admired Karl Marx. Some of the things she and other progressive teachers said reminded me of what we were encountering in seminary. Except, unlike my anti-Christian professors in college, those pushing a similar agenda in seminary camouflaged it underneath a veneer of Christianity. Chapel messages were filled with social justice rhetoric. I remember one speaker telling future pastors: "If caring about justice makes you a liberal, then I'm here to say that God himself is a liberal and you better become one."

Likewise, blog posts hosted, promoted, and sponsored by the seminary pushed the narrative that "white brothers and sisters" needed to "repent" for things like "silence and lack of participation in racial reconciliation." Of course, something as small as working for a company with only "white leadership" may qualify as complicity. Students were also encouraged to interpret "through the eyes of other ethnicities," glean positively from postmodern thinkers like Jacques Derrida, as well as read books shot through with critical race theory, like *The New Jim Crow* by Michele Alexander.

The relatively new "Kingdom Diversity" department hosted talks on kneeling at football games, taking down Confederate monuments, and honoring people like black liberation theologian James Cone. In one semester, three statements condemning Donald Trump or the alt-right originated or were heavily supported by administration and faculty members. Yet I could not remember one statement, other than perhaps the Manhattan Declaration, that anyone in school leadership signed to oppose threats streaming from the left during Obama's presidency.

The impact on the student body was obvious. Mostly young and idealistic aspiring church leaders absorbed what they heard both on campus and in some of their classes. I observed and heard about previous political conservatives who became progressives, and then started liberalizing their theology, during the course of their time at Southeastern. In one class I remember a student publicly condemning "the folks back home" for their disapproval of the NFL because it allowed what seemed to them like disrespect for the American flag. He went on to say that Christians should apologize for the holocaust. I thought the professor would surely correct this misguided student for his ignorance and arrogance but instead the teacher nodded along and expressed approval. Something was changing, and I knew it was not the Bible or me.

At one of the largest evangelical seminaries, well within the boundaries of the Bible Belt, I felt like an outsider. Not just because of my political conservatism, but also my theological convictions. Since that time, I have taken different positions, pursued new areas of study, and moved to different regions of the country, but the battle remains the same. Most of us can now clearly see the attacks on objective truth, the created order, natural affection, impartial justice, and the gospel of grace are not going away any time soon. Even within Christian ministries where members are free to disagree on "secondary matters" such as eschatology, creationism, and predestination, they are frequently bound by an often-unspoken rule not to publicly question the social justice movement.

That is exactly what this book is about though—questioning the social justice movement. After I asked my professor what was happening to our campus, I wanted to know what could be done about it. His advice was to first be a good student—to learn, grow, and use whatever platform I had, even if it was simply talking with classmates, loving others and telling the truth. Today, I am passing this advice on to you. The first stop in fighting against the social justice movement is understanding what it is. That is the primary purpose of this book. The second step is loving others and telling the truth. May God bless you as you learn, grow, and contend for the faith once delivered.

CHAPTER 1
THE HISTORY OF SOCIAL JUSTICE

In Birmingham Alabama, on June 1, 2019, the largest Protestant denomination in the United States, the Southern Baptist Convention, approved a resolution endorsing two modern social justice teachings, critical race theory and intersectionality, as "analytical tools" which could "aid in evaluating a variety of human experiences" so long as they were "subordinate to Scripture."[1] Pastor John MacArthur, a popular evangelical leader outside the denomination, predicted the SBC's demise since the "majority" approved of using "external cultural cues" to interpret "the Bible."[2] James Lindsay, a secular expert on critical theory, concurred stating that the move invited "a huge wooden horse outside [the] door" that would be used as an "eisegetical tool."[3] A writer for *The Federalist*, a politically conservative news source,

---

1. "On Critical Race Theory And Intersectionality," SBC, June 1, 2019, https://www.sbc.net/resource-library/resolutions/on-critical-race-theory-and-intersectionality/.

2. John MacArthur, *John MacArthur Beth Moore Go Home*, interview by Todd Friel, Audio, October 18, 2019, Reformation Charlotte, https://www.youtube.com/watch?v=NeNKHqpBcgc.

3. James Lindsay [@ConceptualJames], 2019, "I don't know much or care much about your theological details, but I can tell you that Resolution 9's invitation of CRT and intersectionality as analytical tools (whether subordinate to Scripture or not) is a huge wooden horse outside your door.," July 26, 2019, 12:53 p.m., https://twitter.com/ConceptualJames/status/1154796848516882433; James Lindsay [@ConceptualJames], 2019, "Southern Baptist Convention. They're currently blowing up over what is called "Resolution 9," which is a call to insert critical race Theory and intersectionality into their official doctrine as an eisegetical tool.," July 26, 2019, 11:09 a.m., https://twitter.com/ConceptualJames/status/1154770807324848128.

stated: "The Southern Baptist Convention is being infiltrated by an ideology that is antithetical to the Christian religion."[4] Yet, most messengers representing the denomination did not see the problem.

Pastor Tom Ascol, one of the dissenting voices at the convention, believed people were "played" because they "didn't understand" what they were voting for.[5] Yet, since the recent increase in social justice rhetoric inspired by the Black Lives Matter movement, it now apparent that many professing evangelicals embrace some of the core assumptions of modern social justice theory.

The Gospel Coalition, an popular reformed evangelical organization, hosted a lament session where influential evangelicals denounced white privilege and systemic racism in both the country and the church.[6] Phil Vischer, the creator of the popular Christian children's show *Veggie Tales*, argued in a viral video that racism was normative in the United States.[7] Most of his information came from Michelle Alexander's revisionist work *The New Jim Crow*, which drew directly from critical race theorists like Derrick Bell and Mari Matsuda.[8] J.D. Greear, the former president of the Southern Baptist Convention, proclaimed the phrase "Black Lives Matter" to be a "gospel issue" and moved to retire the use of both the name of the denomination and the gavel used to preside over meetings by associating them with slav-

4. Matthew Garnett, "In Last-Minute Move, Southern Baptist Convention Supports Anti-Christian Racial Identity Politics," *The Federalist*, June 18, 2019, https://thefederalist.com/2019/06/18/last-minute-move-southern-baptist-convention-supports-anti-christian-racial-identity-politics/.

5. Tom Ascol [@tomascol], 2019, "Yeah. I couldn't help myself & the mic was hot. I think you are exactly right. People didn't understand. The resolution should never have been presented, in my estimation., June 13, 2019, 12:59 p.m., https://twitter.com/tomascol/status/1139215726395449344; David Shannon, *By What Standard? God's World… God's Rules* (Founders Ministries, 2019), 00:02, https://founders.org/cinedoc/.

6. Staff, "Simulcast Video: Lament and Prayer for Racial Justice," *The Gospel Coalition*, June 20, 2020, https://www.thegospelcoalition.org/video/simulcast-video-lament-and-prayer-for-racial-justice/.

7. Phil Vischer, "Racism Video Transcript w/Citations," *Holy Post*, June 19, 2020, https://www.holypost.com/post/racism-video-transcript-w-citations.

8. Barry Latzer, "Michelle Alexander Is Wrong about Mass Incarceration," *National Review*, April 4, 2019, https://www.nationalreview.com/magazine/2019/04/22/michelle-alexander-is-wrong-about-mass-incarceration/; Michelle Alexander, *The New Jim Crow: Mass Incarceration in the Age of Colorblindness* (The New Press, 2020), 280, 305, 319.

ery.[9] These examples only illustrate the tip of an iceberg that includes many denominations, seminaries, Bible schools, ministries, and individual Christian leaders who take it upon themselves to show solidarity with the latest incarnation of the social justice movement.

Despite new terminology such as "get woke," "decolonize," and "mansplain," the current call for social justice is not a recent phenomenon. It is a repackaged configuration of egalitarian ideas heavily influenced over the past century by postmodern and Marxist derivatives. Because groups as diverse as traditional socialists, secular New Left scholars, progressive religious leaders, and today's critical theorists all appeal to the principle of "social justice" in furthering their agendas, the various movements and contributions that fall under the umbrella of the term's modern usage make it difficult to define.

In 1971, political philosopher John Rawls released the popular book *A Theory of Justice*, which conceived of social justice as the kind of benefit allocating system reasonable people would choose if they did not know what social identity, such as gender or race, they would be born into before their existence. Five years later, economist Friedrich Hayek concluded that "social justice" was a vacuous term used to justify the "re-distribution" of larger shares between unequal social groups.[10] Today, *Oxford Dictionary* defines social justice as "Justice in terms of the distribution of wealth, opportunities, and privileges within a society."[11] This basic understanding developed organically in common parlance over the last century-and-a-half.

Though disagreements over the nature of the social problem, as well as differing solutions, emerge between organizations claiming the mantle of social justice, the commonly shared belief is that disparities in advantages

---

9. Leonardo Blair, "JD Greear Endorses Black Lives Matter as Gospel Issue, Denounces Organization," *The Christian Post,* June 10, 2020, https://www.christianpost.com/news/jd-greear-endorses-black-lives-matter-as-gospel-issue-denounces-blm-organization.html; Sarah Pulliam Bailey, "Southern Baptist President Wants to Retire Famed Gavel Named for Slave Holder," *Washington Post,* June 10, 2020, https://www.washingtonpost.com/religion/2020/06/10/southern-baptist-gavel-greear/; Jonathan Howe, "Greear Announces 2021 Annual Meeting Theme," *Kentucky Today,* September 14, 2020, https://kentuckytoday.com/stories/greear-announces-2021-annual-meeting-theme,27950.

10. Friedrich Hayek, "The Atavism of Social Justice" in *Social Justice, Socialism & Democracy: Three Australian Lectures,* CIS Occasional Papers 2 (Turramurra, N.S.W: Centre for Independent Studies, 1979), 4, 11-12.

11. "Definition of Social Justice by Oxford Dictionary," Lexico Dictionaries (English), accessed September 26, 2020, https://www.lexico.com/definition/social_justice.

between social groups are immoral and must be rectified through some kind of reallocation. It should be noted that before the influence of Karl Marx, the term was rarely used and generally referred to protecting the legal rights of citizens equally.[12] In fact, Roman Catholics had a short history of teaching a type of social justice without advocating redistribution, but they too eventually succumbed to the conventional definition.

Redistributive Justice

Following the Industrial Revolution, Roman Catholic social teaching sought to preserve the natural order which had previously existed through agrarian social bonds and obligations. Neither capitalism's unrestricted "competition of forces," nor socialism's "opposition of classes," was an acceptable philosophy. Instead, a "social justice" concerned with the "common good," was to ensure both the right to private property and a living wage.[13] However, beginning in the 1960s, Catholic teaching started highlighting "economic and social differences" between groups like nations and genders as well as accommodating a more expansive understanding of the state's regulatory role.[14] In 2009, Pope Benedict XVI promoted a "distributive" and "social" justice that supported state imposed "mechanisms of wealth redistribution" including the "worldwide redistribution of energy resources." In his own words, the Pope now also believed in "pursuing justice through redistribution."[15] Though this kind of redistributive justice was not a new idea, it did not originate within Christianity.

Gracchus Babeuf, a socialist and leader in the French Revolution, was the first to clearly and publicly advocate for a version of justice which required state redistribution efforts on behalf of the poor. In 1793, he stated that the

12. Thomas Finch, *Essays on the Principles of Political Philosophy*, (W.G. Whittingham and sold by R. Baldwin, 1812), 109; Caleb Stetson, *A Sermon Preached Before the Ancient and Honorable Artillery Company* (Cambridge: E. W. Metcalf and Company, 1830), 7.

13. Thomas Behr, *Social Justice and Subsidiarity: Luigi Taparelli and the Origins of Modern Catholic Social Thought* (Washington, DC: Catholic University of America Press, 2019), 149-173; Pope Leo XIII, "Rerum Novarum: On Capital and Labor," May 15, 1891; Pope Pius XI, "Quadragesimo Anno," May 15, 1931.

14. Pope Paul VI, "Gaudium et Spes," December 7, 1965; Pope John XXIII, "Mater et Magistra," May 15, 1961.

15. Pope Benedict XVI, "Caritas in Veritate," June 29, 2009.

"right to private property" should be "limited" so as to prevent the "injustice" of depriving certain individuals of "social and economic equality."[16] Babeuf stood on a moral platform built by Jean-Jacques Rousseau, who imagined a world in which an egalitarian utopia replaced traditional hierarchies and maintained itself by means of the "social contract."

Rousseau famously stated, "Man is born free, and yet is universally enslaved."[17] Society itself, he believed, imposed "political inequality" by allocating "different privileges," like wealth, honor, and power, to some and not others. Social institutions promoting inequality justified themselves by appealing to "sacred maxims" and claiming "divine right."[18] In contrast, Rousseau advocated a "social compact," drawing its moral authority from the "general will," which eradicated "personal dependence" and "compelled [citizens] to be free."[19] His goal was to return mankind, as closely as possible, to a "state of nature" in which socially imposed disparities did not exist.

Rousseau's teaching contained three major objectives which have carried through the history of the social justice movement: (1), achieving an egalitarian ideal, (2) dismantling social institutions that prevent its achievement, and (3) implementing force capable of executing the utopian dream. After the French Revolution, these ideas took on various forms and spread to other European countries. By the 1840s, the spirit of revolution filled the Continent. In 1844, August Becker, a German socialist wrote *What do the Communists Want?* identifying the "basic rule" of communism in the phrase, "Each according to his abilities, each according to his needs."[20]

Four years later, during the Revolutions of 1848, Karl Marx and Friedrich Engels published *The Communist Manifesto* in which they used conflict theory to explain economic disparities and called for mechanisms to abolish "bourgeois property" through state control of credit, transportation, and

---

16. Samuel Fleischacker, *A Short History of Distributive Justice* (Cambridge, Mass.: Harvard Univ. Press, 2005), loc 1113-1114, 1133-1137, Kindle.

17. Jean-Jacques Rousseau, *A Treatise on the Social Compact, or, The Principles of Political Law* (T. Becket and P.A. De Hondt, 1764), 2.

18. Jean-Jacques Rousseau, *A Discourse Upon the Origin and Foundation of the Inequality Among Mankind* (R. and J. Dodsley, 1761), 6, 182.

19. Rousseau, *A Treatise on the Social Compact*, 27.

20. August Becker, *Was wollen die Kommunisten?*: Rede (Lausanne, 1844).

production, as well as "free public education."[21] Religion had no place in Marx's framework. He declared, "Saintly socialism is but the holy water with which the priest blesses the fulminations of the aristocrat."[22] As a result, Marx attempted to answer the objection that "communism" would abolish "eternal truths," including "justice." Marx's answer was not to argue for a common transcendent principle of justice compatible with communism, but rather to criticize the established understanding of justice as a form of "exploitation… common to all past centuries."[23] In a way, this is why the alternative phrase "social justice," eventually became popular.

At a time when most people interpreted the world in religious terms, harnessing the concept of "justice" in the cause of egalitarian redistribution made socialism more palatable. It effectively baptized secular redistribution schemes with religious language. In 1888, John Rae, a Scottish journalist, stated: "So firm is the hold taken by the notion that the Socialists are the special champions of social justice, that one of our most respected prelates [The Bishop of Rochester] has actually defined Socialism in that sense."[24] Ten years later, Alfred Russel Wallace, a famous British naturalist, spiritualist, and socialist, told the International Congress of Spiritualists that "charity" had "utterly failed" and it was time to "demand Social Justice."[25]

Socialism by Another Name

In his book *Unjust: Social Justice and the Unmaking of America*, Noah Rothman stated that "social justice" came from "utopian theological movements of the nineteenth century" before becoming "an element of the left's governing program in the mid-to-late twentieth century."[26] Social reform movements

21. Karl Marx and Friedrich Engels, *The Communist Manifesto*, ed. Mark Cowling (NYU Press, 1998), 24, 29.

22. Ibid., 30.

23. Ibid., 28.

24. John Rae, "State Socialism," *The Eclectic Magazine of Foreign Literature, Science,* (Leavitt, Trow, & Company, 1888).

25. Alfred Russel Wallace, "Address by Dr. Alfred R. Wallace," *Light: A Journal of Psychological, Occult, and Mystical Research* XVIII, no. 913 (July 9, 1898). 336.

26. Noah Rothman, *Unjust: Social Justice and the Unmaking of America*, (Simon and Schuster, 2019), 14.

for abolitionism, woman's rights, Anti-Masonry, and temperance, all took an almost revolutionary sense of urgency in the Northern United States. Simultaneously, socialist utopian schemes (like Brook Farm and the Oneida Community) and the influx of socialist immigrants (like August Becker) into the Union Army and American journalism, after the failed 1848 German revolution, prepared the way for both secular and Christian social justice efforts.

Franklin Sprague, a Christian minister in Springfield, Massachusetts, and member of a socialist society called The Connecticut Valley Economic Association, wrote *Socialism from Genesis to Revelation* in 1892. In it, he argued for "Christian Socialism" which he claimed applied Christian ethics to the economy and was the "only basis of peace."[27] Though Sprague wanted to reclaim the term "socialism," he admitted there was "prejudice against the word" and often used the term "social justice" instead. He argued there were two competing visions for the state's role. One was "individual liberty," which protected "individual license, social inequality, and individual tyranny." The other was "social justice" which demanded "the public good."[28]

In 1897, Charles Allan, a contributor to the socialist friendly magazine, *The Arena*, portrayed the Hebrew prophets and Protestant reformers as the first to "define the principles of social justice" by taking "the side of the people against privileged classes."[29] The same year, J. Stitt Wilson, a former Methodist minister, who later became the mayor of Berkeley, California and ran for Congress on a socialist platform, founded The Social Crusade "to preach socialism as the means to realize the vision of a truly Christian society."[30] Wilson described his effort in salvific terms: "The 'Social Crusade' goes forth to give light to them that sit in industrial darkness… . condemn the industrial and commercial iniquities, placing them in the fervent light and heat of the New Social Ethics of Brotherhood and Social Justice; and to call men individually to become saviors and redeemers of their fellowmen,

---

27. Franklin Monroe Sprague, *Socialism from Genesis to Revelation* (Lee and Shepard, 1892), iv, iii.

28. Ibid., 170-172.

29. Charles Allan, "The Influence of Hebrew Thought in the Development of the Social Democratic Idea in New England," *The Arena* (Arena Publishing Company, 1897), 756.

30. Stephen Barton, "J. Stitt Wilson, Berkeley's Socialist Mayor," *Exactly Opposite: The Newsletter of the Berkeley Historical Society* 29, no. 2 (Summer 2011), 1.

and socially to a great salvation." Wilson's aim was to create "the eternal social ideal; the kingdom of heaven on the earth."[31]

In 1910, Thomas Cuming Hall, a professor of ethics at Union Theological Seminary, observed that the same kind of people who became Fabian socialists in England, called themselves "Christian socialists" in the United States. Like their Fabian cousins, Christian socialists sought to gradually enact policies for communal ownership, instead of attempting violent revolution. However, unlike the Fabians, who were humanists, Christian socialists were motivated by "social justice and the kingdom of God."[32] Their justification was different but their goal was similar.

Some of the developing sympathy for socialism in Christian circles resulted from strategic messaging on the part of socialists themselves. Rev. Charles Steltzle, who was appointed by the Presbyterian Church, U.S.A, around this time "to conduct a special mission to working people," found that socialists were sending former ministers and priests throughout the country to serve as "organizers and agitators." They used "religious terminology and appeal[ed] to religious motives, but to the end that an earthly utopia may be set up, and without any reference to the life beyond the grave."[33] Leslie M. Shaw, the former Secretary of the Treasury, expressed his alarm that not only educational, but also religious institutions "trend[ed] toward socialism," or the idea that "men must succeed equally, regardless of aptitude."[34] Christian advocacy for social justice rose in the United States and culminated in the Social Gospel movement of Walter Rauschenbusch.

Rauschenbusch, a Baptist church history professor from Rochester, New York became interested in Fabian Socialism after visiting England in 1891. He eventually promoted a view that embraced the "economic doctrines of Socialism" while repudiating the "atheism, free love, and red-handed vio-

---

31. J. Stitt Wilson, "The Social Crusade," *The New Time: A Magazine of Social Progress* 6 (January 1898), 232.

32. Thomas Cuming Hall, *Social Solutions in the Light of Christian Ethics* (Eaton & Mains, 1910), 197-198.

33. Owen Lovejoy, "In the World of Religious Thought," *Current Literature* XXXVIII, no. 3 (March 1905), 271.

34. Leslie M. Shaw, "Trend of Country Points Towards Socialism, Declares Leslie M. Shaw," *The Gateway: A Magazine of the Times Devoted to Literature, Economics, Social Service* (August 1908), 34.

lence" associated with the broader movement.[35] In 1907, Rauschenbusch published *Christianity and the Social Crisis*, in which he lamented that an individualized "faith in the future life" had "subdued the demand for social justice" in Christianity.[36] In order to Christianize the social order, he advocated "the abolition of unjust privilege."[37]

According to him, powerful men "frustrated the cause of... social justice... in order to hold their selfish social and economic privileges." It was, therefore, the job of Christians following Jesus' example to turn the "energies of religion from the maintenance of conservative institutions to the support of movements for political emancipation and social justice."[38] Rauschenbusch's teaching spiritualized socialist ideas by recasting the gospel as call for social justice. His ideas influenced progressive Christian figures like Reinhold Niebuhr, Martin Luther King Jr., and Desmond Tutu. However, theological conservatives rejected Rauschenbusch's reconfiguration.

Fundamentalists, like Charles Erdman, a theology professor at Princeton Theological Seminary, argued against the Social Gospel. He applied the "social principles of Christ" to the hierarchies of family, labor, and civil relationships while denying the idea of an earthly heaven realized through human effort.[39] Unfortunately, for theological conservatives, while they may have slowed the march toward social justice, they were not able to stop it. As the century unfolded, Rousseau's original paradigm morphed into today's social justice movement and gained greater acceptance within the ranks of American Christianity. The next major development to chart its course came from the father of Cultural Marxism, Antonio Gramsci.

---

35. Walter Rauschenbusch, *Christianizing the Social Order* (London: Macmillan, 1913), 338.

36. Ibid., 18.

37. Ibid., 337.

38. Walter Rauschenbusch, *A Theology for the Social Gospel* (London: Macmillan, 1919), 46, 160.

39. R.A. Torrey, *The Fundamentals - A Testimony to the Truth*, vol. 4 (Rio, WI: AGES Software, 2000), 87-88, 90.

Cultural Marxism

For Gramsci, bourgeois dominance ran deeper than economics. The working class often failed to revolt against their overlords because they consented to the "hegemony," or reigning ideologies manifested in the "political, cultural and moral leadership" of the upper class.[40] From the perspective of "the workers and peasants," it was common sense to remain under the control of the "propertied class and the democratic-parliamentary state" so long as it benefitted them.[41] What they did not realize, according to Gramsci, was that their passivity was the result of values imposed on them through things like libraries, schools, voluntary associations, architecture, street names, and the church.[42]

In order to overturn this complex interdependent web of power, socialists needed to cease contenting themselves to operate within the values of the state and start criticizing the status quo, building their own hegemony, and waiting for the collapse of the old order.[43] Gramsci believed intellectuals could play a pivotal role by helping the members of the oppressed class form a common identity through art, technology, and the creation of new organizations.[44]

From 1926 until his death in 1937, Gramsci, a leader in the Communist Party of Italy, remained in the custody of Benito Mussolini's Fascist government. This event sealed Gramsci's status as a martyr in the cause of revolution and afforded him the opportunity to write the *Prison Notebooks*, where he developed his ideas. Gramsci had a profound impact on New Left intellectuals and 1960s radicals. Rudi Dutschke summed up his strategy in 1967 with the famous phrase, "the long march through the institutions," which Herbert Marcuse of the Frankfurt School described as "working against the established institutions while working within them" and building "counterin-

---

40. Antonio Gramsci, *The Gramsci Reader: Selected Writings*, 1916-1935 (NYU Press, 2000), 423.

41. Ibid., 84.

42. Antonio Gramsci, *Prison Notebooks Volume 2, European Perspectives: A Series in Social Thought and Cultural Criticism* (Columbia University Press, 2011), 53.

43. Gramsci, *The Gramsci Reader*, 87.

44. Stephen Gill, *Gramsci, Historical Materialism and International Relations*, Cambridge Studies in International Relations (Cambridge University Press, 1993), 57.

stitutions."[45] As the 20th century proceeded, Western Marxists like Gramsci drilled deep into culture and identified conditions by which the powerful exerted their dominance.

One of Gramsci's friends, a Hungarian Communist leader named György Lukács, argued that capitalism was actually a reality-altering mindset. He stated, "Not until the rise of capitalism was a unified economic structure, and hence a—formally—unified structure of consciousness that embraced the whole society, brought into being."[46] Capitalism was, essentially, a way of thinking that reduced everything to a disposable commodity from journalism to marriage to human worth itself. However, there was an escape from this mental enslavement. Lukács wrote:

> The knowledge yielded by the standpoint of the proletariat stands on a higher scientific plane objectively; it does after all apply a method that makes possible the solution of problems which the greatest thinkers of the bourgeois era have vainly struggled to find and, in its substance, it provides the adequate historical analysis of capitalism, which must remain beyond the grasp of bourgeois thinkers.[47]

Though both the working and propertied classes lived within the "reality" of "capitalist society," capitalism used the "motor of class interest to keep the bourgeoisie [mentally] imprisoned." The working class, on the other hand, had the ability to achieve class consciousness and transcend their social dilemma based on their experience of being "more powerfully affected" by social change. Interestingly, Lukács assumed that the working class also needed insights from bourgeois thinkers like Marx, Hegel, and Kant in order to realize their ethical and epistemological superiority.[48]

The significance of Lukács' teaching lies in the fact that he helped make censorship intellectually justifiable as Marxist regimes and organizations restricted viewpoints they believed did not accord to orthodox lower-class perspectives. He also "inspired the writers of the Frankfurt School... to see

---

45. Herbert Marcuse, *Counterrevolution and Revolt* (Beacon Press, 1972), 55.

46. Georg Lukacs, *History and Class Consciousness: Studies in Marxist Dialectics* (MIT Press, 1972), 100.

47. Ibid., 163-164.

48. Ibid., 164, 199.

through the specious abundance of the American dream, to the 'inner' and 'subjective' alienation that was concealed by it."[49] More and more, Western Marxism took on a religious dimension. Only Marxism, an all-encompassing view of reality, held the key for social liberation bound up in the sacred knowledge of the workers. Soon, this kind of profound insight broadened to include identities other than economic classes.

In 1924, the Institute for Social Research, which came to be known as the Frankfurt School, started in Germany. At the inaugural address, the director, Carl Grundberg, announced that he saw Marxism not in terms of party politics, but rather as an ideologically driven "research methodology."[50] This research primarily focused, not on the "economic base," but rather the "political and cultural superstructure of society."[51] Max Horkheimer became the director in 1930 and charged his colleagues to examine the "entire material and spiritual culture of mankind" in order to expose hidden oppression woven into the fabric of society itself.[52] This approach he referred to as critical theory and described "its goal is man's emancipation from slavery."[53]

Horkheimer lamented that a society worshiping success confined "social justice" to issues like "theft and murder" while turning a blind eye to the "universal injustice" surrounding them.[54] He observed that "progress toward utopia [was] blocked" by a system of "social power" that controlled the masses by what he called the "technocracy," which derived from the Enlightenment and reduced objects to mathematical formulas.[55] Along with Theodor Adorno, another member of the Frankfurt School, Horkheimer published *Dialectic of Enlightenment*, in 1947 which argued that "culture now impresses the same stamp on everything. Films, radio and magazines make up a system

49. Roger Scruton, *Fools, Frauds and Firebrands: Thinkers of the New Left* (Bloomsbury Publishing, 2015), 129.

50. Rolf Wiggershaus, *The Frankfurt School: Its History, Theories, and Political Significance* (MIT Press, 1994), 26.

51. Stephen Bronner, *Critical Theory: A Very Short Introduction, Very Short Introductions* (Oxford University Press, 2017), 2.

52. Brian J. Shaw, "Reason, Nostalgia, and Eschatology in the Critical Theory of Max Horkheimer," *The Journal of Politics* 47, no. 1 (1985), 155-156, 170-171; Max Horkheimer, *Critical Theory: Selected Essays*, (Bloomsbury Academic, 1972), 225-227.

53. Horkheimer, *Critical Theory: Selected Essays*, 246.

54. Ibid., 93.

55. Max Horkheimer, *Eclipse of Reason* (Seabury Press, 1974), 127, 186-187.

which is uniform as a whole and in every part."[56] In their view, Western entertainment media deceived the masses by imposing upon them values supporting the myth that they too, could be successful.[57]

Instead of the bourgeoisie oppressing the proletariat, it was producers and advertisers enslaving consumers by using their desires against their own self-interest.[58] Increasingly, the problem with society was not capitalism, in and of itself, but a culture that tolerated and propagated capitalism. The Frankfurt school thus analyzed and uncovered the totalitarianism baked into various aspects of culture—including commerce, education, religion, entertainment, and sexuality—in order to raise awareness and inspire social liberation.

For example, in 1950, Theodor Adorno collaborated on a sociological work entitled *The Authoritarian Personality*, which had a profound impact on the direction of university research. The study suggested that even traits such as "submission to parental authority," a belief in traditional gender roles, family pride, "fear of homosexuality," a strong devotion to Christianity, and the notion that foreign ideas posed a threat to American institutions signaled "implicit prefascist tendencies."[59] As a result of this kind of thinking, some started referring to the Institute's philosophy as "cultural Marxism" in the 1970s since instead of reducing individuals to economic classes, it categorized people according to various oppressed or oppressor behaviors and identities.[60] It was this particular philosophy, combined with postmodernism, that provided the rationale behind the New Left movement of the 1960s and 70s.

Herbert Marcuse is sometimes called the father of the New Left, a movement begun primarily among students who protested for social justice against the oppression of middle-class cultural standards and expectations. In 1965, Marcuse wrote that "the small and powerless minorities... must

---

56. Theodor Adorno and Max Horkheimer, *Dialectic of Enlightenment, Verso Classics* (Verso, 1997), 120.

57. Ibid., 133.

58. Adorno and Horkheimer, 138; Robert Winston Witkin, *Adorno on Popular Culture* (Psychology Press, 2003), 35.

59. Theodor Adorno et al., *The Authoritarian Personality* (Verso Books, 2019), 385, 428, 357, 860, 729, 108, 224.

60. Peter Ludz, *The Changing Party Elite in East Germany* (MIT Press, 1972), 343; Gregory Baum, *The Social Imperative* (Paulist Press, 1979), 195.

be helped" even if it meant suspending constitutional "rights and liberties." In Marcuse's mind, free speech and assembly should not be allowed for "groups and movements which promote aggressive policies, armament, chauvinism, discrimination on the grounds of race and religion, or which oppose the extension of public services, social security, medical care, etc." In a foreshadowing of today's "political correctness," Marcuse taught that "liberating tolerance" actually meant "intolerance against movements from the Right and toleration of movements from the Left."[61]

Radical Subjectivity

Marcuse gleaned some of his ideas on society in his early years before joining the Frankfurt School while studying under philosopher Martin Heidegger. Heidegger was a member of the Nazi Party and forerunner for what developed into postmodernism. He believed that things were, in part, defined by their context and not simply their essence. For example, factors like time, language, philosophy, and reason itself shaped the identity of individuals. Marcuse put a Marxist spin on Heidegger by applying this idea to the examination of "social arrangements, economic orders, and political formations."[62] Thus, cultural institutions and associations should be defined and described, not according to what they are, in and of themselves, but by their overall effect.

Two influential French Postmodernists, Jacques Derrida and Michel Foucault, took these ideas much further. Derrida, who is often called the father of deconstruction, believed language did not correspond to reality, but rather to itself. This was summarized in his famous statement in 1967 that "there is nothing outside the text."[63] In other words, the symbols which make up language are enmeshed in a sea of other symbols which relate to one another according to the arbitrary "norms and rules" of "institutional structures."[64] To put it another way, meaning was not found in what was

---

61. Herbert Marcuse, "Repressive Tolerance" (1965), https://www.marcuse.org/herbert/ publications/1960s/1965-repressive-tolerance-fulltext.html.

62. Stephen Ronald Craig Hicks, *Explaining Postmodernism: Skepticism and Socialism from Rousseau to Foucault* (Scholargy Publishing, Inc., 2004), 39.

63. Jacques Derrida, *Of Grammatology* (JHU Press, 2013), 163.

64. Jacques Derrida, *Points… : Interviews, 1974-1994* (Stanford University Press, 1995), 28.

said, but rather, by what was meant in accordance with the "hegemony of language."[65] Using certain tools of analysis, many of which were inspired by Marx, Derrida endeavored to deconstruct messages in order to expose the prejudice embedded within them.[66] In so doing, he was actually deconstructing the entire identity of nation-states as represented in their language. Derrida stated himself that "deconstruction" was "a radicalization... of a certain Marxism" and its purpose was political.[67] Because language applied to everything, everything became political.

In the same way Derrida deconstructed language, Michel Foucault deconstructed knowledge by making it dependent on power. Foucault found the classical Marxist critique empty because it failed to understand this reality. He stated that a phrase like, "Liberate scientific research from the demands of monopoly capitalism" may be a "good slogan, but it will never be more than a slogan" because, in actuality, "knowledge and power are integrated with one another."[68] In other words, science itself is embedded in a "discourse," or in a way of thinking which occupies a social "space," approved by the powerful and used to dominate the "bodies" of the less powerful. From the 1960s, to his death from AIDS he contracted at a sado-masochistic bathhouse in 1984, Foucault argued that modern ways of thinking about things like insanity, disease, criminality, and sexuality were all motivated by an exercise in control and oppression. Institutions like hospitals and prisons developed to enforce the prevailing social knowledge.

Foucault became more popular in America than in France and helped propel critical theory into new areas of study. Edward Said used Foucault's power/knowledge dynamic in the creation of postcolonial theory, which traced ways in which Western scholars treated Eastern peoples as a "cultural and intellectual proletariat" through their research.[69] Feminist scholar Kathy Fer-

---

65. Jacques Derrida, *Specters of Marx: The State of the Debt, the Work of Mourning, and the New International* (Psychology Press, 1994), 92.

66. Jacques Derrida, *Positions*, trans. Alan Bass (University of Chicago Press, 1982), 41.

67. Derrida, *Specters of Marx*, 92; Derrida, *Points*, 28.

68. Michel Foucault, *Power/Knowledge: Selected Interviews and Other Writings, 1972-1977* (Pantheon Books, 1980), 52.

69. Robert Young, *Postcolonialism: An Historical Introduction* (Wiley, 2016), 386; Edward Said, *Orientalism* (Knopf Doubleday Publishing Group, 2014), 208; Nicolas Pethes, *Cultural Memory Studies: An Introduction* (Cambridge Scholars Publishing, 2019), 79.

guson appealed to Foucault's theory of "social appropriation" to explain how university programs were instruments of power to reinforce the "bureaucratic discourse."[70] Annamarie Jagose, in her 1996 book on queer theory, stated that "Foucault's writings have been crucially significant for the development of lesbian and gay and subsequently, queer activism and scholarship."[71]

The important thing to remember about the contributions of Foucault and other postmodernists to various critical theories is that they offered Marxists the insights and tools needed to resist and remake the social order in an almost infinite number of ways previously unimagined. Sir Roger Scruton, a conservative political philosopher, pointed out that the thinkers who motivated the New Left treated things like the "patriarchal family," prisons and madhouses, selfish desire, and "heterosexual respectability" as manifestations of the power of the bourgeoisie.[72] Thus, new disciplines which are constantly emerging, are really more complicated versions of Marxism.

For example, one relatively new field, similar to historical revisionism, called "memory studies," draws on concepts like Derrida's "method of deconstruction" to show how cultural memory shapes human psychology.[73] Astrid Erll and Ansgar Nünning describe it as an "approach [which] proceeds from the basic insight that the past is not given, but must instead continually be re-constructed and re-represented."[74] Yet, sub-fields, such as "Africana cultural memory studies" trace the "denial and manipulation of African rights, privileges, and identity" using the "speculative process" of "Black cultural mythology" for the purpose of liberation.[75] What should become apparent is how interrelated, yet infinitely narrow, many of these new disciplines are becoming. Critical race theory and intersectionality are a good example of this.

---

70. Kathy Ferguson, *The Feminist Case Against Bureaucracy* (Temple University Press, 1984), 61.

71. Annamarie Jagose, *Queer Theory: An Introduction* (NYU Press, 1996), 80.

72. Scruton, *Fools, Frauds and Firebrands: Thinkers of the New Left*, 191.

73. Oto Luthar and Heidemarie Uhl, *The Memory of Guilt Revisited: The Slovenian Post-Socialist Remembrance Landscape in Transition* (Vandenhoeck & Ruprecht, 2019), 229; Nicolas Pethes, *Cultural Memory Studies: An Introduction* (Cambridge Scholars Publishing, 2019), 79.

74. Astrid Erll and Ansgar Nünning, *Cultural Memory Studies: An International and Interdisciplinary Handbook* (Walter de Gruyter, 2008), 7.

75. Christel Temple, *Black Cultural Mythology* (SUNY Press, 2020), 118.

In his book *Critical Race Theory: An Introduction*, Richard Delgado credits Marxists, postmodernists and American radicals with helping create critical race theory in the 1970s.[76] Derrick Bell, a law professor at Harvard and one of the founders of critical race theory, believed "progress in American race relations is largely a mirage, obscuring the fact that whites continue, consciously or unconsciously to do all in their power to ensure their dominion and maintain control."[77] The theory's basic teaching is that racism is systemically embedded within the fabric of society and can only be addressed by first interpreting the world through the lens of minority experience. While critical race theory accomplishes deconstruction, the sub-theory "intersectionality" accomplishes construction. It is this element which has become, perhaps, the most important concept for understanding the modern social justice movement.

In 1989, One of Bell's students, Kimberlé Williams Crenshaw, developed "intersectionality" which she said linked "politics with postmodern theory."[78] Crenshaw believed identity politics failed to take into account the existence of groups with more than one socially oppressed identity factor. She argued that someone who was a "woman" and a "person of color" needed unique political representation. James Lindsay and Helen Pluckrose, in their book *Cynical Theories: How Activist Scholarship Made Everything about Race, Gender, and Identity and Why This Harms Everybody*, state that "intersectionality is the axis upon which the applied postmodern turn rotated and the seed that would germinate as Social Justice Scholarship some twenty years later."[79]

Identity politics was developed in the late 1970s by "Black feminists and Lesbians" who wanted to apply Karl Marx's analysis to their own economic situation in which "racial, sexual, heterosexual, and class oppression... [were] interlocking."[80] Crenshaw stated that while "identity-based politics [was]

---

76. Richard Delgado and Jean Stefancic, *Critical Race Theory (Third Edition): An Introduction* (NYU Press, 2017), 5.

77. Derek Bell, *And We Are Not Saved: The Elusive Quest For Racial Justice* (Basic Books, 2008), 59.

78. Kimberle Crenshaw, "Mapping the Margins: Intersectionality, Identity Politics, and Violence against Women of Color," *Stanford Law Review* 43, no. 6 (1991), 1244, 1242.

79. Helen Pluckrose and James Lindsay, *Cynical Theories: How Activist Scholarship Made Everything about Race, Gender, and Identity—and Why This Harms Everybody* (Pitchstone Publishing, 2020), 127.

80. "The Combahee River Collective Statement" (April 1977),

a source of strength" it was "in tension with the dominant conceptions of social justice." The reason was that "social power in delineating difference need not be the power of domination; it can instead be the source of social empowerment and reconstruction."[81] In other words, people do not need to accept the idea that an oppressive culture's negative categorization of certain social groups is something to accept as negative. It could replace Marx's idea of "class consciousness" with an almost infinite number of new groups aware of their oppression and willing to do something about it.

Crenshaw essentially reduced oppression into a monolithic quality some identities possessed more of than others. This served as a glue to help groups with differing identities see themselves as victims afflicted by the same kind of problem. For example, Crenshaw stated that "race can also be a coalition of straight and gay people of color, and thus serve as a basis for critique of churches and other cultural institutions that reproduce heterosexism."[82] The seed Crenshaw sewed at the dawn of the 1990s is now the dominant analysis of the culture's shortcomings in the arena of social justice.

Identifying as a social victim implies a right to social compensation and a need for social representation from allies both in dominant and sub-dominant cultures. The more victimized, the more compensation and representation is required. Therefore, being oppressed or lacking privilege can have its benefits. When informed by critical race theory and its postmodern attachment to finding truth through an oppressed lens, this creates a knowledge hierarchy whereby less social power means greater access to knowledge about systemic oppression in society.

Karl Marx believed the bourgeois were "biased" in their conception of justice because it was rooted in their own dominance.[83] Lukács thought the key to solving the problem of capitalism rested in the knowledge of the proletariat. But it was Crenshaw who established the building blocks for a scale whereby the less privileged someone is, the more right they have to gain a social hearing concerning oppression.

Patricia Hill Collins, a pioneer of intersectionality, refers to this prior-

---

http://combaheerivercollective.weebly.com/the-combahee-river-collective-statement.html.

81. Crenshaw, "Mapping the Margins," 1242.

82. Ibid., 1299.

83. Marx and Engels, *The Communist Manifesto*, 26.

itization as rooted in "standpoint epistemology" which she states "defends the integrity of individuals and groups in interpreting their own experience" by positing that experience provides "distinctive angles of vision on racism, heteropatriarchy, and capitalist class relations for people who are differentially privileged and penalized within such systems."[84] Thus, if someone possesses privilege by nature of being part of a dominant cultural identity, such as a straight white heterosexual Christian male, they are less qualified to address issues of injustice, and their posture should be one of listening. Thus, today's social justice movement, sometimes called "critical social justice," thoroughly combines principles from postmodernism and Marxism in order not only to redistribute material resources, but also power, privilege, and truth itself.

From the streets of France to the heart of American evangelical Christianity, the past three hundred years have seen many changes in the nature of redistributive social justice. Jean-Jacques Rousseau imagined a centralized power capable of achieving egalitarian equality. Karl Marx wanted to accomplish this dream through the redistribution of resources from the haves to the have-nots. Walter Rauschenbusch Christianized socialism under the banner of "social justice." Antonio Gramsci believed it was the cultural hegemony, and not simply the haves, which was actually responsible for oppressing the have-nots. György Lukács saw capitalism as an oppressive mindset and not just an economic system. The Frankfurt School developed critical theory to analyze oppression in cultural institutions. French postmodernists, like Jacques Derrida and Michel Foucault deconstructed language and knowledge as social constructs and power dynamics. Kimbery Williams Crenshaw developed intersectionality, which attempts to construct a new hierarchy based on a matrix of socially constructed victim categories.

Achieving social justice has gone from the redistribution of income to the redistribution of privilege, from the liberation of the lower classes to the liberation of culturally constructed identities, from lamenting victimhood to promoting victimhood, and from changing society through politics to changing politics through society. No social organization remains unaffected. Gramsci's "long march through the institutions" is almost complete. The final stage is to capture the last stand for Western Civilization and conscious of the country—the American evangelical church.

---

84. Patricia Hill Collins, *Intersectionality as Critical Social Theory* (Duke University Press, 2019), 136.

CHAPTER 2

THE SOCIAL JUSTICE RELIGION

THE GOD OF the Bible takes false religion very seriously. The first of the Ten Commandments warns against worshiping other gods. The Old and New Testaments condemn idolatry, sorcery, pagan customs, and false teachings.[1] Syncretism, which seeks to blend different religions, whereby followers of the true God incorporate pagan worship rituals, is also forbidden.[2] Most professing Christians acknowledge the obvious ways in which these principles can be violated, such as through joining cults and participating in the occult. However, many fail to detect how some political movements function as secular religions. Socialist crusades are a primary example and their religious nature has not gone unnoticed.

Secular Faith

As early as 1793, the famous Irish statesman Edmund Burke warned that "Jacobins," a term denoting the "Jacobin Club" behind the French Revolution, sought to replace religion with their own political movement in order "seize social control."[3] In 1840, a tract in Great Britain entitled *Christianity and Socialism: Examined, Compared, and Contrasted* depicted socialism as a "false religion" competing with Christianity to "cure moral and physi-

---

1. Ex 20:4; 22:18; Lev 20:23; Jer 23:16; Col 3:5; Gal 5:20; I Cor 12:2; 1 John 4:1

2. Zeph 1:4-5; 2 Cor 6:14-16

3. Edmund Burke, *The Writings and Speeches of Edmund Burke, The Writings and Speeches of Edmund Burke*, v. 6 (Little, Brown, 1901), 369-370.

cal evil."[4] Around the same time, a Presbyterian pastor in South Carolina accused "atheists, socialists, communists," newly arrived "red republicans," and "jacobins," of attempting to arrange society without regard for God, but instead, "as the machinery of man."[5] Socialism represented a new man-centered attempt to achieve a social equality Christian societies failed to deliver. As Marxism developed and ascended during the 20th century, its essential religious nature became more obvious.

In 1955, the French philosopher Raymond Aron observed that "Marxist prophetism" conformed "to the typical pattern of the Judeo-Christian prophetism." Both condemned the status quo and provided an alternative vision which culminated in a utopia for those who demonstrated obedience to the chosen path through their membership in an exclusive collective group.[6] The answers to fundamental questions of existence and purpose made sense in, and only in, an interlocking all-encompassing paradigm outside of which there was no reality. As Sir Roger Scruton pointed out, Marxism shared the "category of totality" with "traditional religion."[7] Classifying Marxism as both a political and religious arrangement may seem strange to those familiar with Karl Marx's personal feeling toward religion.

Marx famously said religion was "the opium of the people." He followed his statement by claiming that abolishing religion would trade the "illusory happiness of the people... for their real happiness."[8] In Marx's mind, religion was a threat to communism since it reinforced the established political order and convinced the masses to endure temporary deprivations by teaching them to place their hope in an eternal realm. Consequently, revolutionaries inspired by classical Marxism considered their movements incompatible with religion. The church was a tool of the capitalists and Christianity undermined the historical materialism fundamental to Marxism's theory of social devel-

---

4. A. Shepheard, *Christianity and Socialism Examined, Compared, and Contrasted* (J.S. Hodson, 1840), 1, 41.

5. James Henley Thornwell, *The Rights and Duties of Masters* (Press of Walker & James, 1850), 14.

6. Raymond Aron, *The Opium of the Intellectuals* (Transaction Publishers, 2011), 267.

7. Scruton, *Fools, Frauds and Firebrands: Thinkers of the New Left*, 87.

8. Karl Marx, *A Contribution to the Critique of Hegel's Philosophy of Right 1844*, ed. Andy Blunden and Matthew Carmody (1843), https://www.marxists.org/archive/marx/works/1843/critique-hpr/intro.htm.

opment.[9] Thus, classical Marxism competed with traditional religion for the same reason religions competed with one another for popular allegiance.

Marxists did not desire a void to exist where religion once thrived. Instead, they wanted to be the ones to fill that void with their own metaphysical and moral assumptions. That is why communist regimes elevated dictators and party heroes to the level of deity, required subjects to pledge allegiance to the state, and funneled social associations through party channels. Because humans are natural worshipers, suppressing religion in one arena simply ensured it reemerged in another.[10] Some advocates for totalitarian socialism were straightforward about their intentions.

For example, H.G. Wells, a member of the socialist Fabian Society, dedicated himself to achieving a global utopian cooperative called the "Open Conspiracy" which replaced economic, traditional, religious, familial, and national loyalties. Wells described the "Open Conspiracy" as a "great world movement" eclipsing "socialism or communism." He proclaimed, "It will be more than they were, it will be frankly a world religion."[11] In 1940, he called for "outright world-socialism" in the establishment of a "new world order" which he again compared to a "religion."[12] Though most 20th century totalitarian schemes opposed or replaced Christianity, liberation theology represented an effort to infuse Christian teaching with Marxist understandings.

Socialist Syncretism

Rather than using Christianity to bolster the established order, as Marx had feared, liberation theologians created a version of the faith bent on destroying the status quo in favor of an egalitarian social revolution. Relying on insights from Marxism, these innovators crafted "an interpretation of Christian faith

---

9. Nikolai Buharin and Yevgeni Preobrazhensky, *The ABC of Communism: A Popular Explanation of the Program of the Communist Party of Russia*, trans. Eden Paul and Cedar Paul (The Communist Party of Great Britain, 1922), 247-256.

10. Rom 1:19-23

11. H. G. Wells, *What Are We To Do With Our Lives* (Great Britain: Windmill Press, 1931), 126.

12. H. G. Wells, *The New World Order* (London: Secker and Warburg, 1940), 119, 113.

out of the experience of the poor."[13] Perhaps the most famous liberation theologian was Gustavo Gutiérrez, a Dominican priest who learned about Marxism while studying at the Faculty of Theology in Lyons, France.[14]

In his popular 1971 book, *A Theology of Liberation*, Gutiérrez commended Marx's critique of capitalistic society for "pointing the way towards an era in history when man can live humanly." Gutiérrez believed the biblical command to love neighbor was a call to transform social structures which benefitted the few while exploiting certain classes, peoples, and races. Ultimately, Gutiérrez wanted a "radical change in the foundation of society" which challenged "the private ownership of the means of production." This would be accomplished in a Christian framework.[15]

Jesus' vision was to achieve a "different society" where God's love dispelled "all injustice, privilege, oppression, or narrow nationalism." The Gospel included political liberation and solved the problem of social injustice caused by sin. The marginalized, in their moral purity, set the template for this societal salvation as others, whether Christians or not, were converted through working to liberate the poor and oppressed.[16] Liberation theology distorted the reason for Christ's first coming, modified the mission of the church, denied the universality of sin, destroyed traditional Christian teaching on social order, and added to the gospel. It was a version of Christianity conformed to Marxism. Or perhaps, liberation theology can best be summarized as a Marxist faith built on a Christian foundation.

Although liberation theology started in South America in a Roman Catholic context, similar versions arose throughout the world and were adopted by feminists, racial groups, homosexuals and other faiths and traditions.[17]

13. Phillip Berryman, *Liberation Theology: Essential Facts about the Revolutionary Movement in Latin America–and Beyond* (Temple University Press, 1987), 140, 4.

14. Jeffrey L. Klaiber, "Prophets and Populists: Liberation Theology, 1968-1988," *The Americas* 46, no. 1 (1989): 3.

15. Gustavo Gutiérrez, *A Theology of Liberation: History, Politics, and Salvation* (Maryknoll, N.Y.: Orbis Books, 1973), 30, 202,

16. Ibid., 231, 232, 35, 203, 205, 151.

17. Letty Russell, *Human Liberation in a Feminist Perspective—a Theology* (Westminster John Knox Press, 1974); Aloysius Pieris, *Asian Theology of Liberation, Faith Meets Faith Series* (Bloomsbury Academic, 1988); George Edwards, *Gay/Lesbian Liberation: A Biblical Perspective* (Pilgrim Press, 1984); Farid Esack, Qur'an *Liberation and Pluralism: An Islamic Perspective of Interreligious Solidarity Against Oppression* (Oneworld Publications, 1997).

The most influential outgrowth in the United States is black liberation theology which profoundly shaped political figures such as Cornel West, Barack Obama and Raphael Warnock. James Cone, the founder of black liberation theology, may have strayed farther from orthodoxy than Gustavo Gutiérrez.

In his 1969 book *Black Theology and Black Power*, Cone crafted "a theology whose sole purpose [was] to apply the freeing power of the gospel to black people under white oppression."[18] He believed Black Christians could reject the atheism of a Marxist worldview while still utilizing "marxism as a tool of social analysis."[19] In his most popular work, *The Cross and the Lynching Tree*, Cone solidified his views. He believed the "gospel [was] found wherever poor people struggle for justice," Jesus came to earth to show "solidarity with the oppressed," salvation included "black people empowered to love their own blackness," the black victim of lynching "became the most potent symbol for understanding... salvation," and "the cross and the lynching tree interpret each other."[20] Like Gutiérrez and other liberation theologians, Cone gutted Christian teaching while keeping Christian terminology.

Broadly speaking, theologies of liberation were attempts to redefine the faith by conforming it to the revolutionary political impulses of the 1960s. This was not necessarily a new phenomenon. Throughout history examples abound of biblical practitioners importing concepts from other religions to replace fundamental core doctrines. The nation of Israel notoriously adopted Canaanite mythology that subverted their own monotheism, ceremonial law, and ethical commands.[21] During the early church period, heretical Gnostic sects grafted pagan philosophy into their understanding of creation, salvation, and eschatology. Recent history has seen other Christian groups syncretize with collectivist and totalitarian schemes.

For example, during the early twentieth century, the Social Gospel movement merged Fabian socialism with Christian doctrine. Walter Rauschenbusch said he represented men who drew "their economic insight from

---

18. James Cone, *Black Theology and Black Power* (New York: Seabury Press, 1969), 31.

19. James Cone, *Black Church and Marxism* (Institute for Democratic Institutions, 1982), 6-7.

20. James Cone, *The Cross and the Lynching Tree* (Maryknoll, N.Y.: Orbis Books, 2011), 155, 150, 158, 160-161.

21. Deut 12:31; 1 Kings 18:21; 2 Kings 17:33; Zeph 1:5

Socialism, and their democracy and moral ardor from Jesus himself."[22] Not only did this combination redesign Christian social teachings on matters of private property, the role of the church, and the existence of hierarchy but it reshaped the purpose and scope of salvation itself. In Nazi Germany, the German Christian movement, "awakened by the fundamental insights of National Socialism," used higher critical methods to "dejudaize" the faith in order to make it compatible with Nazism.[23] This decision destroyed the inerrancy of Scripture and resulted in a version of Christianity which did almost nothing more than serve as an apologetic for Hitler's agenda. Today, history repeats itself once again as many Christian groups ingratiate themselves to a civil religion dedicated to achieving an egalitarian ideal by deconstructing traditional institutions and forcing equality through mechanisms of the modern state.

Christian Heresy

In some ways, this merger between Christianity and the social justice movement should not come as a surprise. After all, it was professing Christians who originally popularized the term "social justice." It was also in Christian societies that socialist and communist movements first originated. This was not an accident. The late Christian apologist Francis Schaeffer said,

There's only one way to understand utopian Marxianism and that is that it's a Christian heresy." He taught that Marxists used Christianity's "concern for man" as an "individual" to justify their moral claims even though they could not rationalize this concern given their own materialism.[24] In other words, Marxism functioned like a parasite feeding on the ruins of Christian civilization, adopting its templates, using its general themes, and living inside its hollowed-out shell infused with totalitarian assumptions and egalitarian

---

22. Rauschenbusch, *Christianizing the Social Order*, 397.

23. Susannah Heschel, *The Aryan Jesus: Christian Theologians and the Bible in Nazi Germany* (Princeton University Press, 2010), 16, 160, 230.

24. John Gonser and Mel White, *How Should We Then Live? Episode IX: The Age of Personal Peace and Affluence*, Prime Video, Documentary (FilmRise, 1977), 13:31; Francis Schaeffer, *The Francis A. Schaeffer Trilogy: The Three Essential Books in One Volume* (Crossway, 1990), 44.

goals. Many cultural observers are noticing these features in today's social justice movement.[25]

Critical theory expert James Lindsay identified this Christian blueprint when he stated, "Social Justice is ultimately a confessional faith in the Augustinian tradition," meaning that it included confession, conversion, and a liturgy of praise and penance.[26] Joseph Bottum, a social commentator and public intellectual, described the movement as "driven by a spiritual desire" leftover from Protestantism. White guilt, cancel culture, and Twitter replaced original sin, shunning, and church.[27] Author Noah Rothman thought the immutable traits conferred by identity politics combined with social justice imperatives created "something that resembles a religion."[28] Perhaps nowhere is the evidence of underlying religious fervor more noticeable than in the recent Black Lives Matter movement.

Protests inspired by Black Lives Matter broke out around the world—following the passing of George Floyd, a black man, who died after being put in a chokehold as Minneapolis Police detained him for using counterfeit money and resisting arrest. Most media attention surrounding the protests focused on proposed solutions to "systemic racism," such as defunding the police, tearing down historical monuments, and providing reparations for victimized racial groups. Some outlets also reported on the more violent protests which produced property damage and police casualties. Many Amer-

25. Thinkers as varied as Rod Dreher (Orthodox Christian and conservative), John McWhorter (atheist and liberal Democrat), and Douglas Murray (atheist, homosexual, and Neoconservative) all conceive of social justice as a religion. See Rod Dreher, "Social Justice: Our New Civil Religion," *The American Conservative* (blog), July 10, 2019, https://www. theamericanconservative.com/dreher/lgbt-pride-social-justice-our-new-civil-religion/; John McWhorter, "Kneeling in the Church of Social Justice," *Reason* (blog), June 29, 2020, https://reason.com/2020/06/29/kneeling-in-the-church-of-social-justice/; Douglas Murray, "Social Justice" Is a Secular Religion, interview by Zuby, January 5, 2021, https:// lbry.tv/social-justice-is-a-secular-religion:fa6d4e610bbccf73eddb8d5c612c3a1b00aacd70.

26. James Lindsay [@ConceptualJames], 2019, "If people who have taken on their 'antiracism' work actually do like being called racists, in some weird way, especially when they feel called out or do it to themselves, it's because Social Justice is ultimately a confessional faith in the Augustinian tradition.," August 24, 2019, 4:00 p.m., https:// twitter.com/ConceptualJames/status/1165353289703198720.

27. Joseph Bottum, *Wokeness: old religion in a new bottle*, interview by Sean Collins, August 14, 2020, https://www.spiked-online.com/2020/08/14/wokeness-old-religion-in-new-bottle/.

28. Rothman, *Unjust*, 15.

icans were already familiar with the political debate sparked by allegations of police abuse in previous incidents. The difference in this particular scenario was both the massive scale of the movement and what appeared to be the peculiar religious sacraments accompanying it.

Paintings elevating the victims of alleged police brutality to an almost saintlike status appeared around the world while thousands of protestors acted out scenes from their final moments by imitating the victim's body position or chanting their last words.[29] It also became ritualistic for protest attendees to raise black power fists and kneel in unison on the ground. Members of Congress famously donned West African kente cloth as they kneeled for over eight minutes in recognition of George Floyd's death.[30] In a show of submission to the Black Lives Matter narrative, police officers would also often kneel before protestors. Like the officers, white activists sometimes distanced themselves from their own "privilege" by washing the feet and shining the shoes of black people.[31] At one protest in Charleston,

29. Caroline Goldstein, "From Spain to Syria, Street Artists Around the World Are Painting Murals to Memorialize George Floyd—See Them Here," *Artnet News*, June 1, 2020, https://news.artnet.com/art-world/street-art-protest-george-floyd-death-1875156; Zenger [@Zenger], 2020, "Today protesters continue to fill the streets in the tenth day of #GeorgeFloydProtests. For blocks, thousands of activists held a "die-in," where they laid face-down on the ground, representing the manner in which George Floyd died. Filmed by @FordFischer" June 7, 2020, 7:05 p.m., https://twitter.com/Zenger/status/1269767443083296769; Daily Mail, *Portland Moms Sing "hands up, Please Don't Shoot Me" at Black Lives Matter Protest*, 2020, https://www.youtube.com/watch?v=gXTYjpW7tU4.

30. Ironically, kente cloth was "historically worn by the Asante people of Ghana, who were involved in the West African slave trade." See Devon Link, "Fact Check: Yes, Kente Cloths Were Historically Worn by Empire Involved in West African Slave Trade," *USA Today*, June 16, 2020, https://www.usatoday.com/story/news/factcheck/2020/06/16/fact-check-kente-cloths-have-ties-west-african-slave-trade/5345941002/.

31. CNN [@CNN], 2020, "An entire line of officers was seen taking the knee as they faced protesters in Washington state. The attendees of the demonstration, billed as a protest against police brutality, cheered as the officers kneeled.," June 1, 2020, 10:06 a.m., https://twitter.com/CNN/status/1267457457405779968?s=20; "White Cops & Civilians Wash Black Protesters' Feet, Seek Forgiveness," *TMZ*, June 7, 2020, https://www.tmz.com/2020/06/07/white-cops-civilians-wash-feet-black-protesters-north-carolina-forgive/; Keith Griffith, "Chick-Fil-A CEO Urges White People to 'Shine a Black Stranger's Shoes,'" *Daily Mail*, June 20, 2020, https://www.dailymail.co.uk/news/article-8443159/Chick-fil-CEO-urges-white-people-repent-racism-shining-black-strangers-shoes.html.

some white protestors even mimicked abused slaves by showcasing scars on their backs and wearing chains.[32] The parallels were obvious.

Instead of the Christian tradition, which ascribed honor on the basis of virtue and achievement, the social justice movement assigned this quality to members of victimized categories. The veneration of minorities who died at the hands of, or in the custody of, the police rivaled the intensity found in Early Christian martyr cults. However, instead of reaching for a more achievable goal, like emulating a martyr's piety, the social justice faithful could only rehearse the victim's suffering and death. It was in this process that victims paid for the sins of an impersonal and abusive system while members of oppressor groups tried to absolve themselves of complicity. Social justice believers temporarily washed themselves of "whiteness" through public displays of solidarity, whether in physical protests or social media endeavors such as #BlackOutTuesday. Ultimately, it was this sense of shame which created the momentum necessary for the Black Lives Matter movement to go mainstream.

In the Houston neighborhood where George Floyd previously lived, a group of white Christians expressed the heart behind much of the movement when they bowed before a group of black protestors and asked to be forgiven for "years and years of... systematic [sic] racism."[33] In Minneapolis, prayers, baptisms, and worship music rang out near the location of Floyd's death where activists created a shrine referred to as a "church."[34] Protestors made pilgrimages to other "holy sites" including the infamous "CHAZ" commune in Seattle, the Breonna Taylor memorial in Louisville, and the Robert E. Lee monument in Richmond where protestors gathered for speeches, prayers,

---

32. Thomas Novelly [@TomNovelly], 2020, "This group, which self-identified as Stand As One, is now getting yelled at by BLM. The two are arguing about [sic] the their message. The group who brought the slave demonstration were told to leave and exited Marion Square.," June 22, 2020, 6:58 p.m., https://twitter.com/TomNovelly/status/1275201556795854848.

33. "White People Kneel for George Floyd in 3rd Ward Houston," Youtube Video, June 6, 2020, https://www.youtube.com/watch?v=So_PC3rHrXA.

34. Paleo-Economist [@PaleoEconomist], 2020, "Place where George Floyd died is now where baptism takes place and Floyd is now a proclaimed Saint," June 17, 2020, 10:42 a.m., https://twitter.com/PaleoEconomist/status/1273264831777341442; Hebah Farrag, "The Fight for Black Lives Is a Spiritual Movement," *Berkley Center for Religion, Peace & World Affairs*, June 9, 2020, https://berkleycenter.georgetown.edu/responses/the-fight-for-black-lives-is-a-spiritual-movement.

art, music, dance, free food and books, as well as voter registration.[35] It is no wonder that journalist Michael Tracey remarked that every protest he had been to "perfectly mirror[ed] an outdoor Evangelical Christian worship service."[36] There was also a dark side to the movement which paralleled a Christian sense of wrath and judgment.

People started using the term "cancel culture" at the end of 2018, but it did not become popular until the spring of 2020 when individuals, businesses, and institutions faced censorship and destruction on a large scale for failure to comply with social justice driven demands.[37] A digital mob of Twitter users and celebrities smeared Harry Potter author JK Rowling as "transphobic" because she insinuated that menstruation was unique to women. Quaker Oats dumped their Aunt Jemima pancake mix and syrup brand for portraying racially insensitive stereotypes. Ironically, if they asked descendants of actresses who portrayed Aunt Jemima, they would find them proud of their ancestor's performance.[38] Pop Off, an advertising agency, fired music publicist Danielle Reiss simply for posting a picture on social media in which she held a "Make America Great Again" sign. They stated her picture violated their commitment to "equality, inclusion, and kindness."[39] Perhaps small businesses endured the worst effects of cancel culture.

---

35. Ben Dennis 8News [broadcastben_], 2020, "Took a quick lap around the Robert E. Lee monument just now. Plenty of protestors and demonstrators still gather, and listen to prayers and speeches at the foot of the monument after 'Virginia's 5,000 Man March.' @8NEWS," Jun 13, 2020 3:33 p.m., https://twitter.com/broadcastben_/ status/1271888454859796481; Mills Keller [@EdwiredMills], 2020, "Last night the police in Richmond, Virginia tear gassed the crowds around the Robert E. Lee statue — again. This morning, the people were back, registering voters, handing out free water, free food, free books, and lots of positive thinking. #BLM #RVA," Jun 27, 2020 1:12 p.m., https:// twitter.com/EdwiredMills/status/1276926331998044161.

36. Michael Tracey [@mtracey], 2020, "I'm telling you, every protest I've been to so far perfectly mirrors an outdoor Evangelical Christian worship service," Jun 5, 2020, 6:35 p.m., https://twitter.com/mtracey/status/1269035147489411078.

37. "Google Trends: Cancel Culture Search Term," *Google Trends*, accessed February 9, 2021, https://trends.google.com/trends/explore?date=all&geo=US&q=cancel%20culture.

38. Gwen Aviles, "Relatives of Aunt Jemima Actresses Express Concern History Will Be Erased," *NBC News*, June 22, 2020, https://www.nbcnews.com/pop-culture/pop-culture-news/ relatives-aunt-jemima-actresses-express-concern-history-will-be-erased-n1231769.

39. Elle Reynolds, "Music Publicist Says She Was Fired By Email For Attending Trump Rally," *The Federalist*, October 23, 2020, https://thefederalist.com/2020/10/23/ music-publicist-says-she-was-fired-by-email-for-attending-trump-rally/.

At a time when government lockdowns in response to Covid 19 were already destroying small businesses, the social justice movement added an extra barrier. Nini's Deli was the top-ranking restaurant in Chicago in January of 2020 according to Yelp.[40] By June 6, it was permanently closed, boarded up, and graffitied with obscenities, threats, anti-Christian messaging, and social justice symbols associated with Black Lives Matter and the LGBTQIA+ movement. Nini's crime? The owner, Juan Riesco, failed to post a black square on social media for #BlackoutTuesday and voiced disagreement with the anti-family positions of the Black Lives Matter organization. This in turn sparked broken contracts with other businesses, death threats and protests numbering in the thousands outside the restaurant. Juan's family had to flee for their lives to another state in the middle of the night.[41] Of course, these situations only skim the surface of the numerous examples of firings, censorship, violence, and intimidation triggered by failure to meet the demands of the social justice inquisition. For some, the results were even more traumatic.

Multiple videos surfaced of Black Lives Matter activists harassing ordinary citizens at restaurants by requiring reparations or shows of solidarity in a manner almost reminiscent of Maoist struggle sessions.[42] In many cases, protestors brutally beat white people, including the elderly.[43] According to

---

40. Nick Kindelsperger, "Nini's Deli Most Popular Restaurant in Chicago, Says Yelp - Chicago Tribune," *Chicago Tribune*, January 7, 2020, https://www.chicagotribune.com/dining/ct-food-yelp-top-places-to-eat-chicago-ninis-deli-0107-20200107-sz2dq5an2vbincndm3isgmq3qu-story.html.

41. Christian Rangel, "On Nini's Deli," *Medium*, July 8, 2020, https://medium.com/@crangel7/on-ninis-deli-537b5ee7023a.

42. Fredrick Kunkle, "Protesters Target D.C. Diners, Triggering Backlash after Heckling Woman," *Washington Post*, August 25, 2020, https://www.washingtonpost.com/dc-md-va/2020/08/25/dc-protesters-blm-diner-confrontation/; Kristina Wong, "BLM Protesters Harass D.C. Diners, Demand They Raise Fists," *Breitbart*, August 25, 2020, https://www.breitbart.com/politics/2020/08/25/black-lives-matter-protesters-harass-d-c-diners-mexican-restaurant-demand-they-raise-fists/; Gregory Hoyt, "Watch: BLM Terrorizes Patrons, Destroys Restaurant: 'If You Don't Give Us Our Sh-t, We'll Shut Sh-t Down.,'" *Law Enforcement Today*, September 5, 2020, https://www.lawenforcementtoday.com/diners-flee-restaurant-after-blm-terrorizes-rochester-patrons/; Lia Eustachewich, "BLM Protester Caught on Video Harassing Diners Denies Being the 'Aggressor,'" *New York Post*, September 8, 2020, https://nypost.com/2020/09/08/blm-protester-seen-harassing-diners-denies-being-the-aggressor/.

43. "Woman Attacked Outside Rochester Business," *13 ABC WHAM*, May 31, 2020,

some estimates, there was over one billion dollars in property damage and over 2,000 injured police officers in the United States as a result of protests in 2020. The number of officers shot also went up substantially.[44] While it is reasonable to assume that much of the criminal element simply took advantage of the opportunity protests afforded them, it is also true that their justification was rooted in the same moral crusade motivating the entire movement. A kind of "holy war" was acceptable, and perhaps necessary, against an evil white hegemonic power.

Hawk Newsome, president of Black Lives Matter of Greater NY, indicated that violence was unavoidable in the struggle for freedom in an abusive country.[45] Nikole Hannah-Jones, who founded *The New York Times* "1619 Project," stated that property destruction was not violence, but actually a justified rage over disrespect from law enforcement.[46] National Public Radio promoted Vicky Osterweil's book *In Defense of Looting*, which supported attacks on "white settler society" through "broad lawlessness, property

---

https://13wham.com/news/local/woman-attacked-outside-rochester-business; Jackie Salo, "Portland Man Beaten Unconscious by BLM Mob Tried to Stop Mugging, Witness Claims," *New York Post*, August 18, 2020, https://nypost.com/2020/08/18/portland-man-beaten-by-blm-mob-tried-to-stop-mugging-witness-claims/; Andrew Miller, "Videos Capture BLM and Antifa Supporters Assaulting and Robbing Trump Supporters after 'Million MAGA March,'" *Washington Examiner*, November 14, 2020, https://www.washingtonexaminer.com/news/videos-capture-blm-and-antifa-supporters-assaulting-and-robbing-trump-supporters-after-million-maga-march.

44. See Jennifer Kingson, "Exclusive: $1 Billion-plus Riot Damage Is Most Expensive in Insurance History," Axios, September 16, 2020, https://www.axios.com/riots-cost-property-damage-276c9bcc-a455-4067-b06a-66f9db4cea9c.html; Julio Rosas, "Jaw-Dropping: Police Chief Association Releases Number of Officers Injured During Violent Riots," Townhall, November 30, 2020, https://townhall.com/tipsheet/juliorosas/2020/11/30/police-chief-association-releases-jawdropping-numbers-of-injured-officers-during-n2580844; Greg Norman, "Line-of-Duty Police Deaths Surge in 2020 as Coronavirus, Calls to 'defund' Pose Challenge to Officers' Safety," *Fox News*, December 30, 2020, https://www.foxnews.com/us/police-deaths-on-duty-surge-in-2020.

45. Matt London, "Black Lives Matter Leader Justifies Rioting in Interview with Tomi Lahren," *Fox News*, February 12, 2020, https://www.foxnews.com/media/black-lives-matter-president-riot.

46. CBS News [@CBSNews], 2020, "'Violence is when an agent of the state kneels on a man's neck until all of the life is leached out of his body. Destroying property, which can be replaced, is not violence. To use the same language to describe those two things is not moral' -@nhannahjones" on CBS," Jun 2, 2020, 1:55 p.m., https://twitter.com/CBSNews/status/1267877443911778306.

destruction, looting" and possibly even shooting "a few cops and soldiers."[47] In the end, police brutality, economic disparities, and prejudice all emanated from a tendency to "elevate White people over people of Color" in what critical race theorists referred to as "whiteness."[48] And, like sin itself, destroying it sometimes required drastic measures.

In a real sense, believers in Black Lives Matter functioned in an almost Christian way with their own saints, salvation, sacraments, sacred knowledge, sin, and suffering. The chart below outlines some of the parallels to traditional Christian customs and beliefs. (Figure 1)

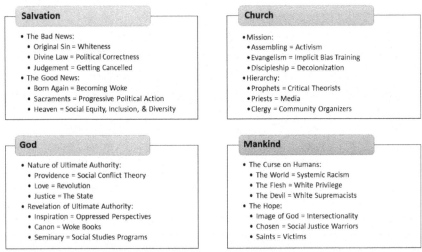

Figure 1

Also, many converts to the Black Lives Matter movement had what seem to be best described as religious conversions. For example, author Jessica Goudeau explained getting "woke," which refers to becoming socially aware of "racism and social injustice," as if it were a born-again experience. Not only did she undergo guilt for her white privilege, but she interpreted her new awareness as "the pathway to liberation from white guilt." This sanctifying process included things like apologizing to black people for inadvertent racism, recognizing one's place in "the system," silently listening to people of

47. Vicky Osterweil, *In Defense of Looting: A Riotous History of Uncivil Action* (New York: Bold Type Books, 2020), 205, 214.

48. Özlem Sensoy and Robin J. DiAngelo, *Is Everyone Really Equal?: An Introduction to Key Concepts in Social Justice Education* (Teachers College Press, 2012), 119.

color, and educating white people on their privilege. Goudeau concluded her testimony with the evangelistic call, "We must devote ourselves to becoming woke."[49] This religious zeal was certainly shared at the highest levels of the movement.

A Faith for All Religions

The founders of the official Black Lives Matter organization saw no conflict between their self-described Marxism, including ties to Chinese Communist Party affiliates, and their religious beliefs.[50] Patrisse Cullors, who first came up with the slogan Black Lives Matter, declared "Our spirituality is at the center of Black Lives Matter."[51] For Cullors this meant practicing "Ifà, a West African Yoruba religion," as well as a blend of "Native American, Buddhist and mindfulness traditions." In an interview, both Cullors and Melina Abdullah, a co-founder of BLM Los Angeles, talked about engaging in ancestral worship, conjuring up the spirits of black victims, and using hashtags like #SayHerName and #BLM to channel spiritual energy.[52] Abdullah also mentioned things like spirit guides, "healing justice," and the divinity of black women on the Black Lives Matter website.[53] Of course, New Age styled beliefs were not the only religious persuasions represented.

BLM Los Angeles chapter included an "interfaith effort" aimed at top-

---

49. Jessica Goudeau, "How to Become Woke," *SheLoves Magazine* (blog), July 19, 2016, https://shelovesmagazine.com/2016/how-to-become-woke/.

50. Yaron Steinbuch, "Black Lives Matter Co-Founder Describes Herself as 'Trained Marxist,'" *New York Post*, June 25, 2020, https://nypost.com/2020/06/25/blm-co-founder-describes-herself-as-trained-marxist/; Trevor Loudon, *Chinese Communist Party Ties to Black Lives Matter* (Choose Freedom, 2020), https://rumble.com/vauw4j-chinese-communist-party-ties-to-black-lives-matter.html.

51. Dan Burke, "The Occult Spirituality of Black Lives Matter," Crisis Magazine, September 8, 2020, https://www.crisismagazine.com/2020/the-occult-spirituality-of-black-lives-matter.

52. Alexander Watson, "BLM Leaders Discuss 'Resurrecting a Spirit So That It Can Work Through Us,'" CNSNews.com, September 22, 2020, https://www.cnsnews.com/article/national/alexander-watson/blm-leaders-discuss-resurrecting-spirit-so-it-can-work-through-us.

53. "'We Keep Us Safe' Community Call Video," *Black Lives Matter*, January 20, 2021, https://blacklivesmatter.com/we-keep-us-safe-community-call-video/; "Black Women Are Divine," *Black Lives Matter*, accessed February 21, 2021, https://blacklivesmatter.com/black-women-are-divine/.

pling "White-supremacist-patriarchal-heteronormative-capitalism" using "spiritual tools."[54] On April 1, 2017, the Black Lives Matter organization hosted a 24 hour event called Sacred Resist which organized "people of all faiths" around the world to "invoke all that is sacred" for their cause.[55] Black Lives Matter also promoted Christian preachers like Michael McBride, Starsky Wilson, and of course Martin Luther King Jr.[56] Not only were they positive about "The Politics of Jesus," but when televangelist Pat Robertson claimed Black Lives Matter was trying to destroy Christianity, the organization demanded an apology and accused him of offending "Christian siblings who are a part of our movement against racial injustice."[57] In a sense, Black Lives Matter was deeply spiritual on its own accord, while at the same time appealing to a wide variety of faiths. Curiously, however, the group's core beliefs contradicted the ethics of most organized religions.

According to the Black Lives Matter website, they not only stood against "state-sanctioned violence and anti-Black racism," but also "heteronormative thinking," "cis-gender privilege," and the "Western-prescribed nuclear family."[58] Many joint Black Lives Matter and LGBTQIA+ protests testify to

---

54. "Who We Are," BLMLA, accessed February 21, 2021, https://www.blmla.org/who-we-are.

55. "Sacred Resist," July 17, 2017, http://web.archive.org/web/20170717201455/https://sacredresist.org/.

56. Black Lives Matter [@Blklivesmatter], 2014, "So grateful for @ReverendStarsky for giving us the WORD. We appreciate you and St. John's United Church of Christ," Aug 31, 2014, 12:02 p.m., https://twitter.com/Blklivesmatter/status/565258579037671430; Black Lives Matter [@Blklivesmatter], 2015, "The Power and Future of Black Faith - Pastor Michael McBride http://ht.ly/IQ27Q #BlackFutureMonth on @blackvoices #BlackLivesMatter," Feb 10, 2015, 4:18 p.m., https://twitter.com/Blklivesmatter/status/506109693484625920; "MLK's Dream. Our Fight.," Black Lives Matter, January 18, 2021, https://blacklivesmatter.com/mlks-dream-our-fight/.

57. Black Lives Matter [@Blklivesmatter], 2014, "By iamreal8 via repostwhiz app: The Politics of Jesus came with full reception of the… http://instagram.com/p/sYNjUSO2BH/," Aug 31, 2014, 6:14 p.m., https://twitter.com/Blklivesmatter/status/506203501945712642; "Statement by Patrisse Cullors, Executive Director, Black Lives Matter Global Network in Response to Pat Robertson's Comments on the Black Lives Matter Movement," *Black Lives Matter*, September 12, 2020, https://blacklivesmatter.com/statement-by-patrisse-cullors-executive-director-black-lives-matter-global-network-in-response-to-pat-robertsons-comments-on-the-black-lives-matter-movement/.

58. "What We Believe - Black Lives Matter," September 17, 2020, http://web.archive.org/web/20200917194804/https://blacklivesmatter.com/what-we-believe/.

the shared partnership existing between the movements.[59] This promotion of sexual deviancy was incompatible with orthodox Christian teaching. Other conflicting assumptions, such as standpoint epistemology, egalitarianism, and Marxism were less overt, but prevalent in the movement as a whole. The website and social media accounts emphasized socially grounded subjective experience, the moral imperative to correct economic disparities, and assigning oppressed or oppressor designations based on conflict theory.[60] For Christians, partnering with the organization, or the narrative of the movement itself, required a certain level of compromise.

Scripture condemned aberrations from heterosexual norms and marital fidelity.[61] Instructions concerning marriage, family, and even social and political relationships assumed the centrality of heterosexual families.[62] Scripture also presented truth as objectively grounded in an invariable, absolute, and unchanging God.[63] The idea that certain demographics, based on social location and lived experience, possessed moral or intellectual superiority, contradicted biblical teaching and resembled ancient Gnosticism. Instead, anyone with God's revelation could access objective truth, regardless of their intersectionality score.[64] Applying justice disproportionally by creating standards which adjusted according to external factors, such as nationality or poverty, was likewise wrong in God's eyes.[65] And, while conflict was part of human history, Scripture taught that all people were under the curse of sin and possessed the capacity for evil regardless of what social group they

59. Sony Salzman, "From the Start, Black Lives Matter Has Been about LGBTQ Lives," *ABC News*, June 21, 2020, https://abcnews.go.com/US/start-black-lives-matter-lgbtq-lives/story?id=71320450.

60. "Why the Movement for Black Lives Is Using the Media to Build Empathy," *Black Lives Matter*, July 19, 2017, https://blacklivesmatter.com/in-the-news-post-title-here-1/; "Black Lives Matter Global Network Responds to the United States Senate Passage of the First Step Act, A Criminal Reform Package," *Black Lives Matter*, December 20, 2018, https://blacklivesmatter.com/black-lives-matter-global-network-responds-to-the-united-states-senate-passage-of-the-first-step-act-a-criminal-reform-package/; "In Response to the State of the Union," *Black Lives Matter*, February 14, 2018, https://blacklivesmatter.com/responsestate-of-the-union/.

61. Lev 18:22-24; Deut 22:5; Rom 1:26-27

62. Deut 24:1-4; Eph 5:22-33; Col 3:18-21; Titus 2:3-5

63. Psalm 119:160; Prov 1:20-23; John 14:6; John 17:17

64. Acts 17:11; Rom 1:19-20; 2:14-15; 2 Tim 2:15

65. Ex 12:49; 23:3; Prov 20:10

belonged to.[66] In addition to functioning as its own religion, the Black Lives Matter movement undermined Christian understandings of sexual ethics, revelation, justice, and the universality of sin.

Woke Christianity

Still, many Christians supported the movement. The *New Yorker* ran a story entitled, "How Black Lives Matter Is Changing the Church" in the late summer of 2020. The author described how the movement "prompted a crisis of moral conscience" for "evangelical and mainstream churches." Young activists opposed what they perceived as the church's failure to "address systemic racial injustice" as well as its "culture of homophobia and misogyny." This helped prompt evangelical leaders to attend protests and even host rallies against racial injustice, a development the author described as "unprecedented."[67] Other mainstream outlets published similar accounts.

Fox News chronicled how Christian leaders stood with the movement by repenting for institutional racism and protesting racial inequality.[68] An article in *The Atlantic* stated, "The evangelical world [was] shifting in ways that would have been unimaginable only a few years ago." Pastors marched with protestors, accepted rebukes from black peers, and started receiving Black ministry leaders in mostly white evangelical circles.[69] Numerous evangelical institutions and churches sponsored lament sessions, drafted statements against systemic racism, and promoted changes in the way their organizations functioned.

Some evangelicals, such as the president of the Southern Baptist Convention, tried to embrace the slogan Black Lives Matter while separating themselves from the organization and their overtly incompatible views on sexuality. One critic of this approach pointed out that Black Lives Matter was

---

66. Rom 5:12; 3:9; Eph 2:1; Is 53:6

67. Eliza Griswold, "How Black Lives Matter Is Changing the Church," *The New Yorker*, August 30, 2020, https://www.newyorker.com/news/on-religion/how-black-lives-matter-is-changing-the-church.

68. Caleb Parke, "Evangelical Leaders Support Black Lives Matter," *Fox News*, June 2, 2020, https://www.foxnews.com/us/evangelicals-support-black-lives-matter.

69. Emma Green, "The Unofficial Racism Consultants to the White Evangelical World," *The Atlantic*, July 5, 2020, https://www.theatlantic.com/politics/archive/2020/07/white-evangelicals-black-lives-matter/613738/.

a clear and defined movement with framers who determined the meaning of their slogan. It was not only confusing to misappropriate their term, but it was also hypocritical, given that evangelicals valued authorial intent and opposed misappropriations of Scripture. In addition, to some extent, evangelicals who attempted this approach inevitably accepted other incompatible assumptions like postmodern standpoint epistemology, Marxist driven social conflict theory, and egalitarianism.[70]

Like cultural Christians before them who created the Social Gospel, the German Christian movement, and liberation theology, evangelicals were once again embracing a religion disguised as a political movement. Many referred to this new development as "woke" Christianity.[71] Not only did it import critical social justice into Christian categories of law, sin, repentance, and forgiveness, but as a result, it introduced a system of works righteousness that stood in contrast to the once-for-all forgiveness provided in the Christian gospel. Some Christian leaders noticed this threat and sounded the alarm.

Prominent radio preacher John MacArthur called social justice "the most subtle and dangerous threat" to the gospel he had ever seen in his lifetime.[72] Voddie Baucham, a popular author and speaker in the reformed evangelical world, called social justice a "cult" that infused familiar Christian terms with new meaning.[73] Other prominent Christian leaders such as apologist James White, pastor Douglas Wilson, and evangelist Paul Washer, signed *The Statement on Social Justice & the Gospel* organized by Michael O'Fallon, the president of Sovereign Nations, and Josh Buice, the president of the G3 conference. The statement clearly identified "postmodern ideologies derived from intersectionality, radical feminism, and critical race theory" as incon-

---

70. A.D. Powers, "Slogans Matter and Sometimes Slogans Divide," *Christian Action League*, June 20, 2020, https://christianactionleague.org/slogans-matter-and-sometimes-slogans-divide/.

71. Thabiti Anyabwile, "Woke Is…," *The Gospel Coalition*, April 16, 2018, https://www.thegospelcoalition.org/blogs/thabiti-anyabwile/woke-is/; Eric Mason, John Perkins, and Ligon Duncan, *Woke Church: An Urgent Call for Christians in America to Confront Racism and Injustice* (Moody Publishers, 2018); Paul Bond, "'Woke' Christians Are Eroding Donald Trump's Base and Dividing the Evangelical Church," October 1, 2020, https://www.newsweek.com/woke-christians-are-eroding-donald-trumps-base-dividing-evangelical-church-1534720.

72. John MacArthur, "Social Injustice and the Gospel," Grace to You, August 13, 2018, https://www.gty.org/library/blog/B180813/.

73. Voddie Baucham, *Fault Lines: The Social Justice Movement and Evangelicalism's Looming Catastrophe* (Simon and Schuster, 2021), 67.

sistent with biblical teaching.[74] However, these efforts failed to impact the majority of mainstream evangelical leaders.

In September 2020, Hillary Clinton said that Black Lives Matter was a "a theological statement" and encouraged the American church to "be a real partner in this moment of moral awakening." There was enough similarity between the Black Lives Matter campaign and Christianity to convince many famous Christians and ministries to partner together. For large portions of mainstream evangelicalism, Clinton's dream was—and is—coming to fruition.

As churches and para-church organizations debate and separate over the issue of social justice in the coming years, students of history should remember the consequences of previous controversies that followed a similar pattern. Students of Scripture should perhaps also recall the words Elijah the prophet spoke to the nation of Israel on Mt. Carmel. A version rewritten for modern application might read: "How long will you hesitate between two opinions? If the Lord is God, follow him; but if *critical theorists*, then follow *them*."[75]

---

74. "The Statement on Social Justice & the Gospel | For The Sake of Christ & His Church," accessed February 22, 2021, https://statementonsocialjustice.com.

75. 1 Kings 18:21 states: "Elijah came near to all the people and said, 'How long will you hesitate between two opinions? If the LORD is God, follow Him; but if Baal, follow him.' But the people did not answer him a word."

CHAPTER 3

THE SOCIAL JUSTICE GOSPEL

IN THE BOOK of Galatians, the Apostle Paul warned Christians against those who preached a different or distorted gospel. The threat to the Galatian church was an attempt to combine faith in Christ with the requirement to keep the law, especially circumcision, for the purpose of justification. Paul argued that trusting in human ability to keep the law was both impossible and dangerous. Instead, he preached the good news that Christ redeemed those who "live by faith" in Him from the "curse of the Law." While the law served to make sinners aware of their need for Christ's atoning work, and as a guide for Christian living, keeping it was never part of the gospel itself.[1] This is why Paul always described the gospel as a work of God on behalf of believers.[2] It was this idea, that the "just shall live by faith" alone, which sparked the Protestant Reformation.[3] Adding the requirements of the law to the gospel created an impossible standard for sinners to reach, denied the sufficiency of the atonement, and destroyed the good news of the gospel. Today, the social justice movement is serving as the occasion for many leaders in churches and organizations with Protestant faith statements to severely blur the line between the law and the gospel.

---

1. Gal 1:8; 2:16; 3:2-3,10-13, 24; 4:21; 5:1-3, 14; 6:2, 13

2. Rom 1:16; 1 Cor 15:1-4

3. Wilhelm Rein, *The Life of Martin Luther*, trans. G. F. Behringer (New York: Funk & Wagnalls, 1883), 38.

An Evangelical Theology of Liberation

It has become very common for social justice advocates in Christian institutions to associate the gospel with working toward certain political ends. The term "gospel issue" is applied to reforming everything from climate change to illegal migration.[4] In an address to the Southern Baptist Convention, J. D. Greear, the president, maintained that "promoting diversity, unity, missions and sex abuse prevention" were all goals the denomination "must continue to pursue in order to put the 'Gospel Above All.'"[5] Most of the content presented at the "Just Gospel" conferences, which are sponsored by prominent evangelical organizations, is also primarily political.[6] The sloppy use of phrases such as "gospel issue," "gospel above all," or "just gospel" to refer to almost anything but the gospel is creating confusion over whether or not the gospel requires human effort.

Russell Moore, a public theologian at *Christianity Today*, delivered a speech in 2018 featured by The Gospel Coalition, entitled "Black & White and Red All Over: Why Racial Justice Is a Gospel Issue." In the speech, given to attendees at the MLK50 Conference, Moore declared that "the American evangelical church need[ed] to be more evangelized" itself.[7] They failed "to be a gospel people" because of their silence in the face of systemic sin such as poor working conditions for sanitation workers, the shootings of African American young men, and present segregation in the church.[8] Moore contrasted this attitude with the example of Martin Luther King Jr. who sacrificed popularity in the short term in order to "preach the gospel in

---

4. Matthew Groves, "Climate Change Is a Gospel Issue. It's Time Christians Acknowledged It," *Baptist News Global*, August 4, 2017, https://baptistnews.com/article/climate-change-gospel-issue-time-christians-acknowledged/; Russell Moore, "Immigration and the Gospel," *Russell Moore*, June 17, 2011, https://www.russellmoore.com/2011/06/17/immigration-and-the-gospel/.

5. Diana Chandler, "'Gospel Above All' Drives Diversity, Unity, Missions, Abuse Prevention," Biblical Recorder, June 10, 2020, https://www.brnow.org/news/gospel-above-all-drives-diversity-unity-missions-abuse-prevention/.

6. "Just Gospel Conference 2020," accessed March 29, 2021, http://justgospelconference.org/.

7. Russell Moore, "Black & White and Red All Over: Why Racial Justice Is a Gospel Issue," The Gospel Coalition, April 5, 2018, 24:00. https://www.thegospelcoalition.org/video/black-and-white-and-red-racial-justice-gospel-issue/.

8. Ibid., 33:10, 19:00, 11:30.

the long run."[9] Presumably, the American Church would become a "gospel people" if they followed Russell Moore's advice by crucifying their "worship styles" and "political alliances," regardless of whether or not they adopted Martin Luther King Jr.'s heretical views or moral indiscretions.[10]

Such teaching confuses the gospel by making the church's ability to keep additional ethical demands, mostly derived from a New Left moral framework, necessary in order to maintain the reality of the gospel's presence in the life of the church. Jesus argued against this kind of moralism in the parable of the Pharisee and the Publican which he directed "to some people who trusted in themselves that they were righteous, and viewed others with contempt." Ultimately, it was not the Pharisee who fasted and tithed, but the tax collector who cried out for God's mercy whom Jesus considered "justified."[11] While Scripture teaches that genuine obedience is evidence of a heart transformed by the gospel, it is never a precondition or basis for Christ's atoning work. Unfortunately, many leaders in evangelical institutions are following the template laid down by liberation theologians by conflating the demands of social justice with the gospel itself.

Walter Strickland, a Southern Baptist professor who is heavily influenced by liberation theology, attaches the work of liberation from systems of oppression to the gospel. In 2016, he told interviewer Lisa Fields that *The Cross and the Lynching Tree* by James Cone was a "beautiful monograph" she needed to read and "be blessed by." He also described *Liberation and Reconciliation* by J. Deotis Roberts, which condemns the "Bible based gospel"

---

9. Ibid., 30:50.

10. Martin Luther King Jr., "What Experiences of Christians Living in the Early Christian Century Led to the Christian Doctrines of the Divine Sonship of Jesus, the Virgin Birth, and the Bodily Resurrection," The Martin Luther King, Jr. Research and Education Institute, 1949, https://kinginstitute.stanford.edu/king-papers/documents/what-experiences-christians-living-early-christian-century-led-christian; "Chapter 26: Selma," The Martin Luther King, Jr. Research and Education Institute, July 7, 2014, https://kinginstitute.stanford.edu/chapter-26-selma; Martin Luther King Jr., "An Address at the Ministers' Leadership Training Program" (Miami, Florida, 1968); The Associated Press, "Boston U. Panel Finds Plagiarism by Dr. King," *The New York Times*, October 11, 1991, sec. U.S.; "Martin Luther King, Jr., A Current Analysis" (Federal Bureau of Investigation, March 12, 1968), 19-20; Martin Luther King Jr., "Family Planning - A Special and Urgent Concern," Planned Parenthood, May 5, 1966, https://www.plannedparenthood.org/planned-parenthood-gulf-coast/mlk-acceptance-speech.

11. Luke 18:9-13

and promotes the teachings of Sigmund Freud and Karl Marx as necessary for Black Theology, as his "favorite theological book of all time."[12] In both cases, Strickland endorsed the works of liberation theologians for how they improved his understanding of the gospel.

J. Deotis Roberts helped him see "the universal imperatives of the gospel" by imagining a more relatable Christ who appeared culturally as "whoever you are wherever you are."[13] James Cone introduced Strickland to the concept of "systemic sin" and opened his eyes "to the idea that Christ is trying to restore brokenness" by addressing issues like racial oppression. In an interview from 2018, sponsored by Southeastern Baptist Theological Seminary, Strickland described James Cone as someone "who wanted to see social vitality of the gospel." In light of Cone's teaching, it was up to believers to "do the work of the social implications [or] the social outworkings of the gospel" which meant understanding "the brokenness of creation" and "fixing it."[14] In direct contradiction to Jesus' teaching, Strickland even described "a summary of the gospel" as "to love God and neighbor," which Jesus clearly taught were actually the two commandments underlying the whole Law and the Prophets.[15] For Walter Strickland, the gospel includes keeping the law.

During a panel discussion on race and justice in the wake of the civil unrest following George Floyd's death, Strickland claimed that American Christians, in order to justify slavery, constructed and passed down a "half gospel" which saved people's souls but neglected "the weighty matters of the law." Instead he advocated the "two parted reality of the gospel" which included accomplishing "justice." Such language is reminiscent of Social Gospel advocates like Richard Ely, who founded the Christian Social Union

---

12. Walter Strickland, "The Balanced Scholar: The Life and Work of J. Deotis Roberts," interview by Lisa Fields, October 14, 2016, https://www.youtube.com/watch?v=vxqW-HQ8Fuc.

13. Ibid.

14. Walter Strickland, From the Lectern - E075 - Remembering James Cone; Part II, interview by Courtlandt Perkins, October 28, 2018, https://www.podbean.com/site/EpisodeDownload/PBC092792H4PE; Walter Strickland, From the Lectern - E074 - Remembering James Cone Part; I, interview by Courtlandt Perkins, October 15, 2018, https://www.podbean.com/site/EpisodeDownload/PBC092E0ZNVYE; James Deotis Roberts, *Liberation and Reconciliation: A Black Theology* (Louisville, KY: Westminster John Knox Press, 2005), xvii, 54.

15. Matt 22:35-40

in 1891 and inspired Walter Rauschenbusch by arguing that "the church had forgotten the true gospel, which included a passion for social justice, and had come to focus solely on the 'one-sided half gospel' of individual salvation." Things like passing good laws and leading crusades against urban living conditions were part of "social salvation."[16] Of course, Ely was also an early progressive who supported eugenics and believed in racial hierarchy, positions which modern progressives reject.[17] Nevertheless, the perception by social justice advocates from Ely to Strickland, that the gospel preached in most evangelical churches is somehow incomplete without the command to work toward social justice, saturates the language of many leaders in evangelical organizations.

Anthony Bradley, a professor of religion at The Kings College and Theologian-in-Residence at a prominent church affiliated with the Presbyterian Church in America, went so far as to say that "evangelicals have never had the gospel" because of their "failure to believe in black equality."[18] One day after the MLK50 Conference, popular evangelical author and speaker, Paul David Tripp, confessed that he was guilty of believing "a truncated and incomplete gospel" which left out "the gospel of [God's] justice."[19] At a recent event sponsored by Trinity Evangelical Divinity School, Raymond Chang, the president of the Asian American Christian Collaborative, stated that white Christian moderates preached a "truncated version of the gospel" that failed to address social disparities. In contrast, he claimed that black slaves had proclaimed a gospel which was "full and robust and perhaps more unblemished and untainted than any version of Western Christianity that we

---

16. Steven Piott, *American Reformers, 1870-1920: Progressives in Word and Deed* (Rowman & Littlefield, 2006), 79-80.

17. Clifford Thies and Ryan Daza, "Richard T. Ely: The Confederate Flag of the AEA?," *Econ Journal Watch 8*, no. 2 (May 2011), 149-151.

18. Anthony Bradley [@drantbradley], 2017, "Here's the problem(and this will be hard): from a black church perspective, evangelicals have never had the gospel. Ever. Read the book "Doctrine A Race." Here then is the actual Q: When will evangelicals embrace the gospel for the first time ever? #BlackChurch," Dec 22, 2017, 1:21 p.m., https://twitter.com/drantbradley/status/944317041497997312; Anthony Bradley [@drantbradley], 2017, "Wilberforce was an abolitionist but also did not believe in the full racial equality of blacks with whites (which was true of almost all abolitionists). Read the book, "The Great White Lie.," Dec 22, 2017, https://twitter.com/drantbradley/status/947593873412550656.

19. Paul Tripp, "My Confession: Toward A More Balanced Gospel," April 5, 2018, https://www.paultripp.com/articles/posts/my-confession-toward-a-more-balanced-gospel.

see today."[20] Dhati Lewis, the Executive Director of Community Restoration with the North American Mission Board, told his podcast audience that the gospel was "not simply a message for the afterlife," but included Jesus' actions in meeting spiritual, emotional, economic, social, and systemic needs. Gospel presentations fell short if they neglected these facets and only focused on how Jesus "died for our sins."[21] One wonders what such voices would say to the Apostle Paul after he described the gospel as simply "the power of God for salvation to everyone who believes" to the church at Rome?[22]

The Social Gospel Reborn

In 1923, J. Gresham Machen, a New Testament scholar at Princeton University, published *Christianity and Liberalism*, in which he addressed a "terrible crisis" over leaders in evangelical churches who were "hostile to the very foundations of the faith" (including rejecting the gospel), but used enough traditional sounding language to avoid detection. Machen said that according to modern theological liberalism, faith is what makes Christ Master in order to seek the welfare of men. In a scathing critique, he wrote, "But that simply means that salvation is thought to be obtained by our own obedience to the commands of Christ. Such teaching is just a sublimated form of legalism. Not the sacrifice of Christ, on this view, but our own obedience to God's law, is the ground of hope."[23] In short, many of today's Christian leaders, influenced by social justice, retain a portion of the legalistic gospel of modern liberalism that underlaid the social gospel movement of a century ago. While they may articulate forgiveness by grace through faith in Christ's finished work, they also add a systemic, institutional, or corporate salvation through law keeping to their gospel message.

In Eric Mason's 2018 book *Woke Church*, the pastor of Epiphany Fellow-

---

20. Ray Chang, "The Kingdom of God & Politics: Daniel (Babylon)" (Trinity Evangelical Divinity School, February 28, 2020), 9:20, https://www.youtube.com/watch?v=oN0iCbbq9rc.

21. Dhati Lewis, "Where Life Exists: What Is Holistic Restoration?," 4:50, https://www.youtube.com/watch?v=PPauoRC2jRg.

22. Rom 1:16

23. J. Gresham Machen, *Christianity and Liberalism* (Grand Rapids: Eerdmans, 1923), 177, 143.

ship in Philadelphia expressed the need to expose how Christians neglected an important aspect of the gospel by failing to "live out the gospel." According to Mason, justification extends beyond "being declared righteous" to include the Christian's responsibility to make "things right on earth." This new understanding of justification prompted him to declare the "white church... heretical" for failing to pursue this goal. The "black church," on the other hand, had a "robust [and] comprehensive view of the gospel" which impacted all of life including "the systems in which the disciple found himself."[24] The term "system," and its derivatives, appeared almost sixty times throughout the book and readers learned that the deconstruction and changing of impersonal systems was part of the gospel.

Mason wrote that the preaching of the gospel message needs to "address the reality of sin on an individual level as well as on a systemic level." Christians would then bring "gospel renewal to systems" by promoting "systemic justice." This kind of action was different than charitably meeting "immediate needs." Instead, the church, as an institution, was expected to challenge things like the criminal justice and educational systems, work against police brutality and racial disparities, and promote black businesses and expanded woman's ministry roles.[25] In essence, the good news of the gospel includes a church that functions directly as an engine for egalitarian social change.

As an example of how a church could fulfill this role, Mason touted Epiphany Fellowship's "Woke Church Interdisciplinary Think Tank" which mobilized professionals "to employ their expertise for gospel change in the world." Ironically, he also cited "Rwanda's Gacaca Court," "South Africa's Reconciliation Committee," and "Germany's De-Nazification Program" as positive models for how the church could accomplish systemic change, "restitute the wrongs of their past," and ultimately, "become a practical prophetic community."[26] Such recommendations raise the obvious questions about whether or not non-believers and secular institutions, without the power of the Holy Spirit, are capable of participating in the work of the gospel as long as they promote social justice.

---

24. Eric Mason, *Woke Church: An Urgent Call for Christians in America to Confront Racism and Injustice* (Moody Publishers, 2018), 43, 45, 99, 126-127.

25. Ibid., 118, 138, 136, 139-140, 161, 154-155.

26. Ibid., 161, 150.

The Whole Gospel

For progressive evangelicals, the idea that the gospel carries a mandate to forward egalitarian goals in systems, structures, and institutions is not a new one. Jim Wallis, Ron Sider, Tom Skinner, John Perkins, and Richard Mouw all promoted secular New Left ideas in evangelical circles during the 1970s.[27] Mouw, who represented the more reformed wing of progressive evangelicalism, appealed to Dutch theologian Abraham Kuyper's conception of "common grace" to justify his social justice infused "full gospel."

For Kuyper, common grace had a redemptive element that enabled unbelievers to exercise "human virtue" and cooperate with believers toward shared political objectives. Mouw used this idea to broaden "Christ's atoning work" to apply to "political institutions and the making of public policy." He stated that the "payment that Jesus made through his shed blood was a larger payment than many fundamentalists have seemed to think... He died to remove the stains of political corruption, and of all forms of human manipulation and exploitation." This meant that the atonement itself could extend to human structures in which the members were not even Christians as long as they were moving in the direction of common grace.[28] Mouw introduced his ideas in his 1973 book *Political Evangelism*.

Like other evangelicals influenced by the secular New Left, Mouw underwent a crisis of faith as a young man when he realized the Christianity he grew up in was not passionate, like his college influences were, about civil rights or opposing the Vietnam War. Before discovering Kuyper's work, Mouw associated with socialists, became an organizer for Students for a Democratic Society and experimented with other religions. After discovering that Christianity could ground his political values, Mouw tried convincing other believers to confront social issues as part of their Christian calling.[29] Practically speaking, incorporating political action as part of the mandate to preach the gospel was effective both in attracting disciples of the New Left, who yearned for a moral foundation for their political views, as well as

---

27. Jon Harris, *Social Justice Goes To Church: The New Left in Modern American Evangelicalism* (Ambassador International, 2020), 21, 40, 51, 63, 69.

28. Ibid., 69-71.

29. Ibid., 37.

in convincing otherwise indifferent Christians to adopt progressive ideas as part of their Christian duty.

Mouw promoted politically progressive causes and candidates from 1972, when he joined "Evangelicals for McGovern," all the way to 2020 when he helped launch "Pro-Life Evangelicals for Biden."[30] He also served as the president of Fuller Theological Seminary for twenty years, contributed to many mainstream evangelical organizations, such as *Christianity Today*, and continues to influence mainstream evangelical leaders such as Tim Keller.

His application of Kuyper's philosophy to politics produced a common perception that the evangelistic task extends beyond helping individual's make peace with God to helping impersonal systems conform to an egalitarian social vision. This approach is similar to liberation theology in how it eliminates the distinction between sacred and secular by advocating a version of salvation which unbelievers can directly participate in. However, Scripture is clear that salvation is only for those "who fear God" and believe in Christ.[31] Some progressive evangelicals saw the obvious problem with Mouw's approach.

Ron Sider, a Messiah College professor who represented the Anabaptist wing of progressive evangelicalism, did not believe in "evangelizing' political structures" or that "salvation" and "redemption" could apply to secular institutions. However, he did argue in his 1977 best seller *Rich Christians in an Age of Hunger* that "structural" sin was responsible for wealth disparities and that Christians should advance the cause of "redistribution of the means of producing wealth." In Sider's mind, social justice was not part of the gospel, but believing the gospel did "necessarily involve" promoting social justice.

At the point of conversion, Christians were required to repent from "the sin of involvement in structural evils such as economic injustice and institutional racism." This particular sin was so broad it even included things like passively belonging to an affluent nation which allegedly "profited from systemic injustice." Author Craig Gay summed up Sider's position well by stating that receiving the gospel also meant "a conversion to a particular kind of [economic] analysis."[32]

---

30. Ibid., 34; "Home | Pro-Life Evangelicals for Biden," Pro-Life Evangelical, accessed April 6, 2021, https://www.prolifeevangelicalsforbiden.com.

31. John 14:6; Acts 4:12; 10:43; 13:34; 1 Tim 2:5

32. Harris, 72-73, 39-42.

Sider believed that evangelicals needed "a more holistic biblical gospel" which was not "unbiblical in its individualism" or "heretical in its separation from a call to costly discipleship." The gospel was more than a "vertical encounter" with God that produces "forgiveness and regeneration." It also "redeemed" horizontal relationships, such as economic, racial, and gender divisions through the witness of the church. Sider even claimed that evangelicals denied the "full biblical doctrine of the atonement" because of a "heretical" failure to embrace Christ's pacifism.[33] For Sider and other Anabaptists influenced by the New Left, the church was responsible to model a "countercultural community" which represented "Jesus' full gospel of the kingdom" including "racial reconciliation" and "economic justice." Failing to model Christ's present "messianic reign" in these ways also meant failing to embrace, and ultimately denying, the gospel itself.[34]

However, Scripture never teaches or implies that believers need to work to maintain the standing before God which Christ achieved for them or the kingdom blessings accompanying Christ's work. On the contrary, the Apostle Paul wrote, in the beginning of his letter to the church at Ephesus, that it was the Father through Christ who freely bestows on believers "every spiritual blessing," positional righteousness, "adoption," "redemption," "forgiveness," knowledge, and "an inheritance." The only instrument Paul mentioned for receiving such blessings was believing the message of the gospel.[35] Even the physical manifestations of the kingdom of God were presented as the work of God himself.[36]

Scripture also distinguishes the gospel from the fruit or evidence that the gospel produces. In Paul's letter to the Galatians, he stated that it was "the gospel which has come to you, just as in all the world also it is constantly bearing fruit and increasing."[37] In the second epistle to the Corinthians, Paul wrote that "if anyone is in Christ, he is a new creature; the old things passed away; behold, new things have come. Now all these things are from God,

---

33. Ron Sider, "Evangelicalism and the Mennonite Tradition," in *Evangelicalism and Anabaptism* (Scottdale, PA: Herald Press, 1979), 151-153, 155-156.

34. Ron Sider, *Good News and Good Works: A Theology for the Whole Gospel* (Baker Publishing Group, 1999), 75-78.

35. Eph 1:3-14

36. Matt 4:23, 9:35

37. Col 1:5-6

who reconciled us to Himself through Christ."[38] The Apostle Peter called Christians to obedience in light of their receiving the gospel, not as way of determining whether the gospel they received was inadequate or false.[39] Conflating the gospel with the fruit of the gospel, like Sider, has become a standard way for social justice evangelicals to frame their agenda. Failure to measure up to often extra biblical and progressive expectations is grounds for failing the test of orthodox belief.

Ron Sider's influence upon mainstream evangelicalism cannot be underestimated. Such names as Russell Moore, David Platt, John Piper, Jonathan Leeman, and Jemar Tisby have all gleaned from his writings.[40] His emphasis on making the church the model and instrument for social change as part of the gospel is often combined with Mouw's emphasis on changing secular social institutions as part of the gospel. In general, most evangelical social justice advocates today blend interpretations of liberation, Kuyperian, and Anabaptist theologies freely and likely without consideration for the progressive evangelicals who first used the Christian gospel to justify New Left ideas within their faith tradition.

Weaponized Apologies

The Apostle Paul condemned all such mechanisms by which humans attempt to contribute their own merits to the accomplishment of Christ when he told the churches of Galatia that "by the works of the Law no flesh will be justified." He went on to state that "if righteousness comes through the Law, then Christ died needlessly."[41] Yet this is what many social justice advocates in evangelicalism teach. They can articulate mankind's need for the grace of God and the exclusivity of faith in Christ for salvation and yet simultaneously apply His atoning work to individuals, the church, and impersonal systems through the ability of humans to keep a New Left derived law. Though Paul

---

38. 2 Cor 5:15-18

39. 1 Peter 1

40. Harris, *Social Justice Goes to Church*, 141-142.

41. Gal 2:16, 21

taught that the gospel of grace left no place for boasting in human accomplishment, this configuration allows for just that.[42]

Jesus warned about this kind of boasting in the Sermon on the Mount. "Beware of practicing your righteousness before men to be noticed by them." He then cited the way the Pharisees sounded trumpets when giving to the poor and called attention to themselves when praying in public places as actions to avoid.[43] In the midst of a scathing rebuke against the scribes and Pharisees Jesus also accused them of being unwilling to live up to their own standards and "do[ing] all their deeds to be noticed by men." Their motive was not loving God, but instead receiving social honor, authority, respect, and position.[44] Today, many social justice advocates display a similar attitude. One way is through weaponized apologies.

In 1940, C. S. Lewis observed a tendency in young English Christians to apologize for foreign policy decisions they were not old enough to participate in but which they presumed contributed to World War II. Lewis quipped that "men fail so often to repent their real sins that the occasional repentance of an imaginary sin might appear almost desirable." Essentially, "the young man who is called upon to repent of England's foreign policy is really being called upon to repent the acts of his neighbour." Pretending to take responsibility for other's failures can actually serve as a clever and prideful way to criticize and single out those who do not engage in the same kind of apology while simultaneously projecting the appearance of personal humility. Lewis wrote that the "charm of national repentance" was how it enabled someone to denounce "the conduct of others... yet feel at the time that [they were] practising contrition."[45] The parallels between what Lewis described and what commonly takes place within the ranks of social justice advocacy are striking.

At the 2019 Cru staff conference, speaker Latasha Morrison led thousands of employees in one of the largest evangelical organizations in a "liturgy" in which they lamented actions like mocking the poor, allowing institutional racism, participating in racial segregation, ignoring the plight of brown and

---

42. Rom 3:21

43. Matt 6:1-5

44. Matt 23:4-6

45. C.S. Lewis, "Dangers of National Repentance (1940)," *Transformation 14*, no. 4 (1997): 10.

black men, and idolizing the nation.[46] In June of 2020, The Gospel Coalition hosted "A Night of Lament for Racial Justice" in which evangelical leaders such as Mark Vroegop, Shai Linne, and David Platt asked for God's conviction, indicted the church's callousness, and confessed things like partiality.[47] In honor of Martin Luther King Jr. Day 2021, Mark Yarbrough, the president of Dallas Theological Seminary, offered an "institutional apology for our past racial sins" in chapel which included slavery, segregation, and continued prejudice. Yarbrough also asked forgiveness for those "suffering" and "wronged" by the institution, though he did not provide any concrete examples.[48]

While there are instances of national repentance in Scripture, they involve present participation in sin, by perpetrators, directed to the Lord, and resulting in forgiveness. Today however, weaponized apologies are often for past, unrelated, or uncharacteristic wrongs, by those not responsible, frequently to other social groups, and perpetually without lasting forgiveness. C. S. Lewis pointed out that "the moment there is reason to suspect that [someone] enjoys rebuking" someone they love, there is reason to doubt the authenticity of their rebuke. Sinful humans generally do not welcome the opportunity to publicly admit actual sin, or the sins of a beloved institution. Yet at the very moment evangelicals are announcing their complicity in racism, so are most secular institutions. That is because weaponized apologies are not actual apologies. Their purpose is to advance accusations that portray others, who fail to apologize, as morally inferior. In a sense, weaponized apologies are a subspecies of the virtue signal.

James Bartholomew, a contributor to British magazine *The Spectator*, coined the term "virtue signalling" in 2015 to describe "the way in which many people say or write things to indicate that they are virtuous" in an often-subtle way and without "doing anything virtuous."[49] The term is most

---

46. Latasha Morrison, "General Session" (Cru19, Colorado State University, July 21, 2019), 1:25:00.

47. A Night of Lament for Racial Justice (The Gospel Coalition, 2020), 17:00, 19:00, 23:50. https://www.youtube.com/watch?v=gwJiHMz0E7g.

48. Mark Yarbrough, "Racism, Repentance, and Moving Forward in Hope: A Statement from Dallas Theological Seminary" (Voice, January 18, 2021), https://voice.dts.edu/article/racism-repentance-and-moving-forward-in-hope/.

49. James Bartholomew, "I Invented 'Virtue Signalling.' Now It's Taking

often applied to progressives who use circumstances to publicly announce their commitment to egalitarian principles with little to no sacrifice on their part. They generally live in a world where bravery and courage involve offending those who cannot harm them to appease those who can. Unfortunately, this tendency toward empty boasting is not unique to secular progressives. Leaders at evangelical institutions are also joining the bandwagon, often dragging their understanding of the gospel with them.

Days after Rayshard Brooks was killed by Atlanta police when he failed a sobriety test, resisted arrest, and tried to escape while shooting a Taser at one of the officers, Passion City Church hosted a discussion on racial injustice with popular pastor Louie Giglio, CEO of Chick-fil-a Dan Cathy, and rapper Lecrae.[50] Both Giglio and Cathy lamented the church's involvement in sanctioning "legalized oppression" and "racial discrimination" as well as existing racial disparities.[51] Throughout the conversation, the speakers proposed vague solutions, such as rebuilding "the system," taking responsibility, fighting for African Americans, and listening to black voices.[52] However, their greatest demand was for white people to feel the pain of black people. Cathy declared, "it has to hurt us" and "there's got to be an emotional response." Giglio agreed—"we've got a ways to go to get to this point of empathy."[53] All of this was sanctioned by Giglio's understanding of the gospel.

He announced, in a way reminiscent of liberation theology, that "the gospel [was] a justice proposition at its core" because it involved the murder of a man "in broad daylight in the street... suffocat[ing] for the weight of our sin." The similarities between Jesus and figures like George Floyd were unmistakable. Pastor Giglio also believed the proper motivation for marching in protest was because "the gospel proposition" and "the justice proposition" were "woven together from the beginning." The "blessing of the cross" meant

over the World," The Spectator, October 10, 2015, https://www.spectator.co.uk/article/i-invented-virtue-signalling-now-it-s-taking-over-the-world.

50. Michael King, "Man Dies after Being Shot by Atlanta Police at Wendy's Drive-Thru," 11 Alive, June 13, 2020, https://www.11alive.com/article/news/crime/man-critically-injured-after-being-shot-by-atlanta-police-during-traffic-stop/85-b7faf368-0315-4db5-b863-4d6a4c140784.

51. The Beloved Community - Dan Cathy, Lecrae, Louie Giglio (Passion City Church, 2020), 14:40, 18:15, 18:40, https://www.youtube.com/watch?v=xEuI-03Jcc4.

52. Ibid., 15:10, 17:30, 18:15, 26:05.

53. Ibid., 18:15, 33:25, 34:20.

that Christians needed to die to themselves and live for God when it came to racial injustice.[54]

In a grand display meant to signify this reality, Cathy arose from his seat in the middle of the discussion, knelt down at Lecrae's feet, and proceeded to shine his shoes as a sign of his own willingness to contribute "personal action." However, instead of thanking Cathy, Lecrae asked for "some stock in Chick-fil-a."[55] In an interview the next day, the Platinum-selling rapper told a reporter that he disapproved of Giglio and Cathy's "virtue signaling" and thought apologies and attempts to appear "multicultural" were inadequate in dismantling white supremacy.[56] Their emotional expressions may have gained them respect with some viewers at a time when most leaders were universally condemning alleged racism and distancing themselves from social groups in which racism was thought to be acceptable. However, Lecrae wanted policies and programs aimed at eradicating disparities, not activities which only accomplished making people feel like they accomplished something.[57] Lecrae made good on his commitment later that year when he took social justice thinking to its logical conclusion and campaigned in the Georgia senatorial election for Democrat candidates Raphael Warnock and Jon Ossoff.[58]

Virtue signaling is attractive because at a very minimal cost it allows one to justify himself while disassociating from the sin of others. Jesus described the Pharisees in a similar way as "those who justify [themselves] in the sight of men." But he also warned that what "is highly esteemed among men is detestable in the sight of God."[59] Though the Pharisees appeared righteous, they were "full of hypocrisy and lawlessness" and not able, based on their righteousness, to "enter the kingdom of heaven."[60] Though they paid lip

54. Ibid., 45:30, 20:15.

55. Ibid., 39:50.

56. Chuck Creekmur, "Lecrae Responds To 'White Blessings' Controversy, Apologizes and Explains Exactly What 'Had Happened,'" *All HipHop* (blog), June 17, 2020, https://allhiphop.com/features/lecrae-addresses-racist-comments-by-atlanta-pastor/.

57. Ibid., 50:35.

58. Warnock, Ossoff Rally in Atlanta on 1st Day of Georgia Early Voting (Atlanta, 2020), https://www.youtube.com/watch?v=67a8QT5KUeQ.

59. Luke 16:15

60. Matt 23:28, Matt 5:20

service to God's law, they lacked a sense of proportion toward what they chose to obey and what they chose to ignore. In vivid imagery Jesus declared: "You blind guides, who strain out a gnat and swallow a camel!"[61] Today, many social leaders try to appear righteous by announcing their commitment to egalitarian values during news cycles which target alleged bigotry while simultaneously ignoring, downplaying, or nuancing greater evils perpetuated by political progressives. The way many evangelicals influenced by social justice reacted to the civil unrest precipitated by the narrative accompanying George Floyd's death is illustrative.

J. D. Greear, the president of the Southern Baptist Convention, announced his intention to "retire the Broadus gavel" used to preside over convention meetings since 1872 because it was "named after a Southern Baptist who owned slaves." In Greear's mind, retiring the gavel was part of "keeping the Gospel above all."[62] However, when asked how Christians should react to the protests, including the "looting and violence and rioting," his answer was to rush to "empathy" instead of a "solution."[63]

Ligon Duncan, the chancellor of Reformed Theological Seminary, passionately campaigned to replace the Mississippi State flag because of its Confederate imagery. When asked what motivated him, he claimed the flag was part of a "huge lost gospel opportunity" tied to Jim Crow, lynching, and opposition to civil rights even though its original intent was memorializing the "valor and courage" of "brave men."[64] However, when publicly addressing the "riot[s] & protest" he expanded culpability to include the entire nation and focused instead on the "staggering magnitude of injustice against African-Americans."[65]

---

61. Matt 23:24

62. J. D. Greear, "FIRST PERSON: It's Time to Retire the Broadus Gavel - Baptist Press," Https://Www.Baptistpress.Com/, June 11, 2020, https://www.baptistpress.com/resource-library/news/first-person-its-time-to-retire-the-broadus-gavel/.

63. J. D. Greear and Bryan Loritts, How should Christians respond to the protests happening across the country?, interview by Matt Love, June 4, 2020, https://jdgreear.com/podcasts/how-should-christians-respond-to-the-protests-happening-across-the-country/.

64. Ted Ownby et al., *The Mississippi Encyclopedia* (University Press of Mississippi, 2017), 437.

65. Ligon Duncan [@LigonDuncan], 2020, "O God, we humble ourselves before you because of our national sins. And in this time of riot & protest we especially lament the "staggering magnitude of injustice against African-Americans." O Lord, forgive &

In a similar way, Matt Chandler, the popular pastor of the Village Church in Dallas, Texas, framed George Floyd's death as part of a "demonic evil" which characterized the United States and posted a black square on his Instagram account.[66] In order to "uproot" racism, Chandler asked his followers to reject "a truncated understanding of the gospel" which failed to "expose injustice."[67] However, when addressing the "violent riot[s]," Chandler scolded those who "point[ed] out all the flaws in this current movement" while abandoning the church's responsibility to protest against injustice.[68]

All three leaders—Greear, Duncan, and Chandler—cooperated with the same inconsistent narrative the Black Lives Matter movement promoted. The highly publicized altercations between police and black individuals in 2020 were the result of systemic racism stretching back to the early years of the United States. Rectifying the problem involved sacrificing understandings, traditions, symbols, and relics of the past. The nationwide violence, looting, and vandalism accompanying the riots should be rationalized in light of systemic racism. The major difference between social justice advocates in evangelicalism and those in the secular world was the way they portrayed their motive.

Greear, Duncan, and Chandler, publicly depicted their anger over systemic racism, and their symbolic and ostentatious gestures to combat it, as rooted in a concern for the gospel itself. Yet, in comparison, they minimized anger over the resulting murder, theft, and property destruction by not publicly condemning the riots in the same terms or connecting opposition to them with the gospel. Not surprisingly, all three managed to condemn the Trump supporters, protesting for election integrity, who illegally entered the

---

change us. In wrath, remember mercy.," May 31, 2020, 9:58 a.m., https://twitter.com/LigonDuncan/status/1267093192371056641.

66. Matt Chandler [MattChandler74], 2020, "If not now when? Pray and fast, lament, act.," June 2, 2020, https://www.instagram.com/p/CA7x4AwlruZ/.

67. Matt Chandler [MattChandler74], 2020, "Pray, fast, lament, and go to work," May 27, 2020, https://www.instagram.com/tv/CAswwmIlXlg/; Matt Chandler [MattChandler74], 2020, "If not now when? Pray and fast, lament, act.," June 2, 2020, https://www.instagram.com/p/CA7x4AwlruZ/.

68. Matt Chandler [MattChandler74], 2020, "A word from Ephesians 1:18. Preaching through the Prayers of Paul. This was out of sermon 1 of what we're calling "Petitioning the Possible"," June 8, 2020, https://www.instagram.com/tv/CBMt_TlNQ-/.

national capitol building on January 6, 2021.[69] Some protests were more important to condemn than others.

The Gospel According to Critical Race Theory

Unlike the stability of God's moral law, which reflects His unchanging character and is codified in a fixed canon of writings, man's moral views are subject to fluctuation. The social justice movement has undergone significant revisions and taken different forms in only the short span of a century. This makes the codification of a stable moral law difficult. Social justice is easier to define in reference to the hierarchies it is deployed against and the egalitarianism it is intended to accomplish. Nevertheless, in its current form, most social justice advocates incorporate key philosophical and moral assumptions stemming from critical race theory.

In *Critical Race Theory: An Introduction*, authors Richard Delgado and Jean Stefancic identify at least seven basic teachings which characterize the ideology. First, racism is normative; second, race is a social construct created in order to allocate privilege (social construction thesis); third, white privilege maintains white dominance; fourth, color blindness keeps minorities in subordinate positions; fifth, majority groups tolerate advances for racial justice only when it benefits them (interest convergence); sixth, voices of color have access to special knowledge (standpoint epistemology); and seventh, history should be reinterpreted according to minority experience (memory studies).[70] Perhaps no one, working in a conservative evangelical institution, has done more work to integrate the philosophy and ethics of critical race theory with the Christian gospel than Jarvis Williams.

---

69. J.D. Greear, [@jdgreear], 2021, "(2/10) What happened yesterday was a disgrace, not only to democracy, but to the ordinance of submission to which God has called us in relation to our earthly leaders.," Jan 7, 2021, 3:10 p.m., https://twitter.com/jdgreear/status/1347274333677379588; Ligon Duncan [@LigonDuncan], 2021, "#OTD, January 6, 1066, Harold Godwinson seized the throne of England. We know how that turned out.," Jan 6, 2020, 9:22 p.m., https://twitter.com/LigonDuncan/status/1347005745838100482; In an Instagram video, Matt Chandler reacted to the controversial events on January 6 stating, "It's just so sick," and "His kingdom doesn't look like storming the capitol." See Matt Chandler, [mattchandler74], Jan 6, 2021, https://www.instagram.com/tv/CJuZraegnyh/

70. Richard Delgado and Jean Stefancic, *Critical Race Theory: An Introduction*, Second Edition (NYU Press, 2012), 15, 21, 87-88, 27, 165, 10, 24.

Dr. Williams is a professor of New Testament interpretation at The Southern Baptist Theological Seminary in Louisville, Kentucky which serves as the flagship seminary for the Southern Baptist Convention. In a 2017 interview featured on The Gospel Coalition website, Williams shared that Richard Delgado's *Critical Race Theory: An Introduction* was a book he "wish[ed] every evangelical Christian would read" because of how "behind" evangelicals were "on critical race discussions."[71] Williams credited some of his own understanding of race to critical race theorists and believed the ideology could give Christians "insights" on the nature of "race and racism."[72]

A side by side comparison of Williams's teaching with Delgado and Stefancic's version of critical race theory indicates that Williams has produced a Christianized version of the ideology. He has taught that "every ethno-racial group outside of faith in Jesus Christ

is a racist group," that "Race… is a construct that people created for the advancing of a racist agenda," that "privilege" and "whiteness" keep "minorities without a voice" in the Southern Baptist Convention, "that the color blind theory of race is a myth," that "certain predominately white churches" want a "multiethnic church" as long as they are not required to share "privilege and power with… black and brown people," that "white" people need to learn the "narrative" of "different ethnic" and "marginalized" groups to access certain truth, and that "Critical Race Theory and Social Identity Theory are helpful tools for understanding identity formation in the NT."[73]

---

71. Jarvis Williams, On My Shelf: Life and Books with Jarvis Williams, interview by Matt Smethurst, February 28, 2017, https://www.thegospelcoalition.org/article/on-my-shelf-life-and-books-with-jarvis-williams/.

72. Jarvis Williams, [@drjjwilliams], 2015, "@Irwyn Many of the key writers are self-proclaimed far left thinkers. Yet, they have helped me understand race, even when I disagree w/ them," July 21, 2015, 2:36 p.m., https://twitter.com/drjjwilliams/status/623562320300670977; Jarvis Williams, [@drjjwilliams], 2015, "My Christian brothers and sisters should become familiar w/ critical race theory. I don't agree w/ everything in theory. But offers insights," July 21, 2015, 2:17 p.m., https://twitter.com/drjjwilliams/status/623557382761783296; Jarvis Williams, [@drjjwilliams], 2015, "If we want to convince people that racism exists, we must help them to understand what race and racism are. Critical race theory can help us," July 24, 2015, 1:22 p.m., https://twitter.com/drjjwilliams/status/613759069745188864.

73. Jarvis Williams, "The Intersection of Race, Gospel, and Racial Reconciliation in Paul's Theology," 6 https://www.scribd.com/document/424625751/Williams-Class-Notes; Jarvis Williams, "Jarvis Williams: How the Gospel Addresses Racial Issues," YouTube Video, 2016, 00:50, https://www.youtube.com/watch?v=-qh7NenWRdI; Kevin Jones

For Williams, teachings consistent with critical race theory were necessary for accomplishing "racial reconciliation," which he called a "gospel
issue," a doctrine as important as "penal substitution," and part of the "gospel
message" which "Jesus preached," as evidenced by His healing gentiles and
including them as part of the church.[74] The reason most Christians did not
work toward Williams's version of racial reconciliation was "because of an
incomplete understanding of both the gospel and race."[75] Williams even
used his "7 year old son" as an example of someone who did not fully understand the gospel because he still believed in "the color-blind theory of race."[76]

Though Williams taught that the "unification of all things in Christ"
included the blessing of "racial reconciliation," Southern Baptists still needed
to "work toward removing the stain of racism from their churches, from
their homes, and from every aspect of SBC life."[77] For Williams, the gospel
included more than the "entry language" of "justification by faith" but also
incorporated "maintenance language" which told "one how to live in the
power of the Spirit."[78] He concluded that one could believe "all of the right

and Jarvis Williams, *Removing the Stain of Racism from the Southern Baptist Convention:
Diverse African American and White Perspectives* (B&H Publishing Group, 2017), 101;
Jarvis Williams, [@drjjwilliams], 2015, "Critical race theorists have shown in a compelling
way that the color blind theory of race is a myth!," June 4, 2015, 12:44 p.m., https://
twitter.com/drjjwilliams/status/616643915354087424; Jarvis Williams et al., "Removing
the Stain of Racism from the Southern Baptist Convention Panel," (2017), 34:20,
https://www.youtube.com/watch?v=imN8SvGTWz4; Jarvis Williams, Tips for Ongoing
Racial Learning and Growing, (VergeNetwork, 2020), 2:20, https://www.youtube.com/
watch?v=qdxn7rGl8p4; Jarvis Williams, [@drjjwilliams], 2015, "Critical Race Theory
and Social Identity Theory are helpful tools for understanding identity formation in the
NT. Great resources available," July 2, 2015, 12:25 p.m., https://twitter.com/drjjwilliams/
status/616643915354087424.

74. "The Intersection of Race, Gospel, and Racial Reconciliation in Paul's Theology,"
12; "Removing the Stain of Racism from the Southern Baptist Convention Panel," 57:25;
Removing the Stain of Racism from the Southern Baptist Convention, 85.

75. *Removing the Stain of Racism from the Southern Baptist Convention*, 84.

76. Jarvis Williams, [@drjjwilliams], 2015, "My 7 year old son currently believes
the color-blind theory of race. As he understands the gospel more & gets older, will
realize he's wrong," August 28, 2015, 11:28 p.m., https://twitter.com/drjjwilliams/
status/637285754767548416.

77. "The Intersection of Race, Gospel, and Racial Reconciliation in Paul's Theology,"
9; *Removing the Stain of Racism from the Southern Baptist Convention*, 74.

78. "The Intersection of Race, Gospel, and Racial Reconciliation in Paul's Theology,"
1, 9.

things about justification by faith" and still disobey the gospel by failing to believe the right things about racial reconciliation.

For example, William's taught that the Apostle Peter's error in obscuring the gospel by compelling "gentiles to live like Jews" in Galatians 2:14 was not "not because Peter misunderstood justification by faith," but rather because he advocated a "Torah-observant-Gentile-exclusive gospel." Nevertheless, the Apostle Paul clearly attributes Peter's error to causing confusion over "justifi[cation] by faith in Christ and not by the works of the Law."[79] Similarly, Williams highlighted how Paul did not mention justification by faith in his discussion of the gospel in 1 Corinthians 15:1-8.[80] Yet, Paul clearly conveyed the concept of justification in verse three when he wrote, "Christ died for our sins according to the Scriptures." Unfortunately, Williams's version of the gospel is merged with a law influenced by critical race theory.

Historic Christian confessions clarified the role of good works in the lives of believers. The Westminster Confession of Faith states, "These good works, done in obedience to God's commandments, are the fruits and evidences of a true and lively faith."[81] The Heidelberg Catechism also referred to good works as the "fruits" of a Christian "faith."[82] However, as theologian Sinclair Ferguson observed, "good works... never in any way become part of our standing as justified before God."[83] Justification is separate from the process of sanctification, wherein Christians are "strengthened... to the practice of true holiness."[84] It is on this point that the theology of the Reformation deviates from both the Roman Catholic Church and much of social justice influenced Christianity.

In both cases, the lines between justification and sanctification are blurred and keeping the law is commonly associated with helping to ground

---

79. Gal 2:14-16

80. "The Intersection of Race, Gospel, and Racial Reconciliation in Paul's Theology," 11.

81. "The Westminster Confession of Faith," Ligonier Ministries, 16.2, https://www.ligonier.org/learn/articles/westminster-confession-faith/.

82. "Heidelberg Catechism" (Christian Reformed Church in North America, 2011), Q & A 86, https://www.crcna.org/welcome/beliefs/confessions/heidelberg-catechism.

83. Sinclair Ferguson, *The Whole Christ: Legalism, Antinomianism, and Gospel Assurance—Why the Marrow Controversy Still Matters*, (Crossway, 2016), 12.

84. "The Westminster Confession of Faith," 13.1.

justification. Also, like the Pharisees, they both require adherents to follow an extra-biblical law of their own making. The only way for the Pharisees to maintain their social status was to establish a new metric by which they focused on keeping a set of man-made traditions instead of following God's commands.[85] In the 2018 book, *Removing the Stain of Racism from the Southern Baptist Convention*, Jarvis Williams, along with many prominent Southern Baptists, including Al Mohler and Danny Akin, advised readers on keeping the gospel's demand to work against the racism which, they maintained, characterized the denomination.[86]

In William's chapter, he gave fifteen "exhortations" for "removing the stain of racism from the SBC." His instructions included silently "listening" to voices of color, "support[ing] multiethnic church plants," attributing racism as the cause of certain disparities within the denomination, applying anti-racist principles to a broad spectrum of minority groups, sharing "leadership and influence" platforms with "black and brown" people, interacting more with "black and brown believers," recognizing the wisdom of "black and brown people," organizing conferences "predominately led by black and brown individuals," erasing "images of a white Jesus, white disciples, and all-white children learning at the feet of Jesus," "incorporat[ing] more black and brown people into [denominational] leadership," rejecting color blindness, promoting diversity in personal lives, "befriend[ing] black and brown people lacking celebrity status," recognizing as legitimate the mistrust black and brown people may have toward evangelicals on "race relations," and remembering that "black and brown Southern Baptist churches need to become more diverse and inclusive as well."[87]

Many of William's admonitions are generally represented in the multitude of sermons, lectures, and books promoting strategies for accomplishing an ideal multiethnic church that, generally, attribute white supremacy to be the major obstacle in its achievement. However, as Rick Hardison, a Southern Baptist pastor, argued in his dissertation critiquing the multiethnic church model, "the Bible contains no particular command, theological reason or normative pattern that calls churches to strive to become as ethnically

---

85. Mark 7:9

86. *Removing the Stain of Racism from the Southern Baptist Convention*, 27.

87. Ibid., 99-105.

diverse as their communities."[88] Simply put, Williams's exhortations are extra-biblical and informed more by an understanding of critical race theory than an understanding of God's commands.

In the epistle to the Galatians, the Apostle Paul categorized two different groups of people responsible for advancing "another gospel" which incorporated elements of the law. The first group he referred to as "false brethren" who desired to "boast."[89] Ultimately, they stood "accursed" before God.[90] In common usage, the term translated as "false brethren" referred to "traitors within a city who allowed the enemy to sneak into the city and survey its defenses."[91] Paul used similar language in his epistle to the Philippians when he referred to the "false circumcision" and "enemies of the cross of Christ whose end is destruction."[92] Those who actively fuse the demands of social justice with the gospel fall into this category.

A second category referred to those who, like the Apostle Peter, "stood condemned" because, out of fear, they were not "straightforward about the truth of the gospel." Paul described them as hypocrites whose motive was avoiding "persecution."[93] They were not "accursed," but they were guilty of enabling those who were.[94] Christians who are orthodox in their own personal theology but fail to publicly oppose "another gospel" and knowingly platform those who promote another gospel are in this category.

Al Mohler, the president of the flagship seminary of the Southern Baptist Convention and known for his political and theological conservatism, has changed some of his public views as American culture has shifted Left over the past several years. In 2014, Mohler "repented of denying the existence

88. Richard Hardison, "A Theological Critique of the Multi-Ethnic Church Movement: 2000 - 2013" (The Southern Baptist Theological Seminary, March 31, 2015), 14, https://repository.sbts.edu/handle/10392/4853.

89. Gal 2:4, 6:13

90. Gal 1:8

91. Bob Utley, *Commentary: Paul's First Letters: Galatians I and II Thessalonians* (Bible Lessons International, 1998), 39.

92. Phil 2:18-19

93. Gal 2:11-14; 6:12

94. Gerhard Kittel, Gerhard Friedrich, and Geoffrey W. Bromiley, *Theological Dictionary of the New Testament: Abridged in One Volume* (Wm. B. Eerdmans Publishing, 1985), 122.

of [same-sex] sexual orientation."[95] The next year, he condemned reparative therapy treatment for homosexuality, after signaling support for it eleven years prior.[96] His views on racism also adjusted in ways which match New Left thinking.

In a 2018 interview with Jarvis Williams, Mohler stated that his "biblical theology [was] in a very different place than it was in 1995" when he was part of an effort by Southern Baptists to separate themselves from racism of the past by passing a resolution apologizing for complicity in slavery and racism.[97] At the time, Gary Frost, the denomination's first African American vice president accepted the apology on behalf of black Christians.[98] Since then, Mohler came to realize that it was impossible to separate the denomination from complicity in racism. He stated:

> It's going to take everything we got in the gospel and the Scriptures to escape the trap of history. But we can't just draw a line. We're going to need to deal with it. We're going to have to confront it. We're going to have to recognize the word "stain" is exactly the right word. The stain that we're going to carry as a denomination forever til Jesus comes. But it's a stain that if we deal with rightly can actually show the power of Christ[99]

In Mohler's view, racism would always characterize the Southern Baptist Convention on some level despite efforts to eradicate it. In contrast, the

95. Albert Mohler, "Sexual Orientation and the Gospel of Jesus Christ," Albert Mohler, November 13, 2014, https://albertmohler.com/2014/11/13/sexual-orientation-and-the-gospel-of-jesus-christ.

96. Bruce Schreiner, "Reparative Therapy Criticized by Southern Baptist Theologian," *The Associated Press*, October 5, 2015, http://web.archive.org/web/20151007202446/https://bigstory.ap.org/article/260d8379ea7c49f98ff01b1a29fc0eb1/reparative-therapy-criticized-southern-baptist-theologian; Albert Mohler, "Psychologists Join the Gay Marriage Bandwagon," Albert Mohler, August 3, 2004, https://albertmohler.com/2004/08/03/psychologists-join-the-gay-marriage-bandwagon.

97. "Removing the Stain of Racism from the SBC," 2018 CP Stage (Cooperative Program, June 19, 2018), 3:15, https://vimeo.com/275937055.

98. John Dart, "Southern Baptists Vote to Issue Apology for Past Racism," *Los Angeles Times*, June 21, 1995, https://www.latimes.com/archives/la-xpm-1995-06-21-mn-15534-story.html.

99. "Removing the Stain of Racism from the SBC," 4:30.

Apostle Paul wrote that those "justified in the name of the Lord Jesus Christ" were not defined by their former sin patterns.[100]

Later that year, Mohler declined to sign *The Statement on Social Justice & the Gospel* because he could not "associate with any assertion that we do not have a massive problem in the society and in the church with claims of [white] racial superiority."[101] Around the same time, he released a *Report on Slavery and Racism in the History of the Southern Baptist Theological Seminary* in which he lamented how Southern Baptists were still "guilty of a sinful absence of historical curiosity" by ignoring the "deep racism" in the story of their denomination.[102] In his contribution to *Removing the Stain of Racism from the Southern Baptist Convention*, during the same year, Mohler characterized the United States as "conceived in racism" though "every society show[ed] the stain [of racism] in every epoch."[103] More recently, he said there existed a "real problem of the sin of racism in the United States and in every structure in the United States."[104] Mohler's assessment of the continuing prevalence of racism is similar to the way socialists in the 1970s, such as Michael Harrington, diagnosed a "new racist dispensation" unrectified by civil rights legislation and resulting from "the racist economic structure."[105]

In the aftermath of the Ferguson, Missouri grand jury decision to acquit officer Darren Wilson in the shooting of Michael Brown, Mohler reinforced the idea that the incident was connected to a greater narrative of police mistreating "communities of color" who were not "just making these problems up." He stated that Christians should be foremost in considering "the accusations and concerns coming from the African-American community" and implied the nation's "system of justice" was not fair on "the questions of

---

100. 1 Cor 6:9-11

101. Albert Mohler on Social Justice and the Gospel at The Southern Baptist Theological Seminary (SBTS) Chapel (The Southern Baptist Theological Seminary, 2018), 21:40, https://vimeo.com/289925393.

102. "Report on Slavery and Racism in the History of the Southern Baptist Theological Seminary," SBTS, December 12, 2018, https://www.sbts.edu/southern-project/.

103. *Removing the Stain of Racism from the Southern Baptist Convention*, 62-63.

104. Albert Mohler, "Baptist 21 Virtual SBC Panel 2020," 2020, 35:20. https://www.youtube.com/watch?v=xYzhkleFrjY.

105. Michael Harrington, *Toward a Democratic Left: A Radical Program for a New Majority* (Penguin Books, 1969), 74–75.

race and the law."[106] After the death of Breonna Taylor, Mohler contrasted his "helpful" encounters with Louisville police with those in "African-American neighborhoods… who are afraid when they see blue lights behind them."[107] When George Floyd died, Mohler signed a statement connecting the situation to "inequitable distributions of justice" like segregation and slavery.[108] Though no evidence existed suggesting any of these police encounters were motivated by racial animosity on the part of the officer, Mohler connected them to what he believed were pervasive systemic disparities.

For Mohler, racism was the "antithesis of the gospel" and a "heresy" no one could believe while simultaneously "rightly present[ing] the gospel" because it denied "the full power of his substitutionary atonement." Yet, at the same time, he thought the "racist defenders of slavery" who founded his seminary affirmed "Baptist orthodoxy," "preached the gospel of Jesus Christ to all people," and held to the same gospel he himself believed.[109] This tension in Mohler's understanding of the gospel came out again in 2019 when he recommended an article coauthored by Jarvis Williams and "centered in the gospel." It argued that the gospel was meant to reconcile ethnically diverse groups, that "racism and white supremacy" were opposed to the gospel, and that Christians should use the gospel to combat racism. Yet it also claimed that Christians need to be aware of their "complicity in racism" through their

---

106. Albert Mohler, "The Ferguson Moment—A Moral Test for the Nation," November 26, 2014, https://albertmohler.com/2014/11/26/the-ferguson-moment-a-moral-test-for-the-nation.

107. Albert Mohler, "The Rule of Law and the Demands of Justice: Ahmaud Arbery, Breonna Taylor, and the Questions That Must Be Answered," May 14, 2020, https://albertmohler.com/2020/05/14/rule-of-law.

108. "Southern Baptist Leaders Issue Joint Statement on the Death of George Floyd," May 30, 2020, https://www.baptistpress.com/resource-library/news/southern-baptist-leaders-issue-joint-statement-on-the-death-of-george-floyd/.

109. Albert Mohler, "The Table of the Nations, The Tower of Babel, and the Marriage Supper of the Lamb: Ethnic Diversity and the Radical Vision of the Gospel of Jesus Christ" (Audio, The Southern Baptist Theological Seminary, February 3, 2015), 6:40, https://equip.sbts.edu/chapel/the-table-of-the-nations-the-tower-of-babel-and-the-marriage-supper-of-the-lamb-ethnic-diversity-and-the-radical-vision-of-the-gospel-of-jesus-christ-2/; Albert Mohler, "The Heresy of Racial Superiority—Confronting the Past, and Confronting the Truth," June 23, 2015, https://albertmohler.com/2015/06/23/the-heresy-of-racial-superiority-confronting-the-past-and-confronting-the-truth; Williams, *Removing the Stain of Racism from the Southern Baptist Convention*, 62; "Report on Slavery and Racism in the History of the Southern Baptist Theological Seminary."

"silence about racism" and failure to "apply the whole gospel." Mohler agreed with William's approach when he wrote "the gospel needs to be preached to the church" due to its complicity in "racial injustice and systemic wrong."[110]

Mohler seemed to both affirm and deny the legitimacy of the gospel of Christians who held to orthodox belief yet also participated, on some level, in cultures or systems that were somehow connected to a version of racism. Such confusing and contradictory language echoed the words of the Apostle Paul who accused Peter of being "not straightforward about the truth of the gospel" which Peter knew.[111] Like many social justice advocates in evangelical institutions, Mohler promotes the multi-ethnic church model which connects the work of promoting diversity to the gospel.

At Southern Seminary's 2015 convocation, Mohler announced that authentic "gospel churches" would "look more and more like a changing demographic map" and that "if the church gets [ethnic diversity] wrong," they were "getting the gospel wrong."[112] In 2018 he stated his intention for Southern Seminary to increasingly represent "many races and nations and ethnicities" as part of looking "more like the people born anew by the gospel."[113] For the Southern Baptist Convention, he wanted transformation through "removing racism stain by stain as a sign to the world of the power of the gospel."[114] As a result, Mohler opposed displaying the Confederate Battle

110. Albert Mohler, [@albertmohler], 2019, "The right way to confront racism is biblical and theological and centered in the gospel of Christ. A timely word from @drjjwilliams and @curtiswoods4 in @CTmagazine," August 6, 2019, 6:53 p.m., https://twitter.com/albertmohler/status/1158873835938156547; Jarvis Williams and Curtis Woods, "Jesus, Deliver Us from This Racist Evil Age," *Christianity Today*, August 9, 2019, https://www.christianitytoday.com/ct/2019/august-web-only/deliver-us-from-this-racist-evil-age.html; Williams, Removing the Stain of Racism from the Southern Baptist Convention, 64.

111. Gal 2:14

112. Mohler, "The Table of the Nations, The Tower of Babel, and the Marriage Supper of the Lamb: Ethnic Diversity and the Radical Vision of the Gospel of Jesus Christ," 6:10; Andrew Smith, "Mohler Emphasizes Ethnic Diversity as Gospel Imperative at Southern Seminary Convocation," Southern News, February 5, 2015, /2015/02/05/mohler-emphasizes-ethnic-diversity-as-gospel-imperative-at-southern-seminary-convocation/.

113. "Report on Slavery and Racism in the History of the Southern Baptist Theological Seminary."

114. Williams, *Removing the Stain of Racism from the Southern Baptist Convention*, 63.

Flag and using the Broadus Gavel during the denomination meetings, and he established a five million dollar scholarship for African American students.[115]

Some have speculated that Mohler's posturing is part of the denomination's "incredible strategy to become more diverse" in order to survive changing demographic trends and the scrutiny of social justice advocates.[116] Because of Mohler's history in promoting orthodoxy, it is hard to understand his newfound desire to use the gospel as a way to justify the manufacturing of ethnic diversity. The way in which he endorses figures like Russell Moore and Jarvis Williams, who do advocate another gospel, also causes confusion.[117] Yet as Paul confronted Peter for behaving like the Judaizers, so too must Christians today confront both those who add social justice imperatives to the gospel and those who obscure the gospel.

There is only one gospel of grace carried down through the annuls of church history and inherited by Christians in modern times. It is the same regardless of the demands of social and political movements. Human efforts cannot be added to it, nor can it be added to human efforts as a way to earn God's favor. It serves a different purpose than the law of God. While good works should showcase the evidence of a heart transformed by the gospel, they can never serve as part of the basis for that transformation. While many of today's social justice advocates in evangelical institutions desperately want to connect the gospel to their secular political ideas, the reality is, there is no way to accomplish this task without creating what the Apostle Paul called "another gospel."

115. Mohler, "The Heresy of Racial Superiority"; Carol Kuruvilla, "Evangelical Leader Calls On Denomination To Retire Gavel Named For Slaveholder," *Huffington Post*, June 11, 2020, https://www.huffpost.com/entry/broadus-gavel-southern-baptist-jd-greear_n_5ee261fdc5b6fdbc0a8e5448.

116. Adam Greenway and Chuck Lawless, The Great Commission Resurgence: Fulfilling God's Mandate in Our Time (B&H Publishing Group, 2010), 95.

117. Albert Mohler, [@albertmohler], 2018, "Just realized that today is @drmoore's 5th anniversary as president of the @ERLC. Congratulations on an historic half-decade of leadership, and prayers for many more.," June 1, 2018, 9:58 p.m. https://twitter.com/albertmohler/status/1002731238162161670.

CHAPTER 4
SOCIAL JUSTICE EPISTEMOLOGY

ON A HOT July Saturday morning in 2019, thousands of staff workers from one of the largest Christian organizations gathered in the Moby Arena at Colorado State University to hear keynote speaker Sandra Van Opstal teach on worship and justice. Van Opstal, who had been on staff with the sponsor organization Cru for fifteen years, was also heavily involved with social justice initiatives such as Chasing Justice, Evangelicals for Justice, and the Christian Community Development Association.[1] In the opening to her speech, she told the story of studying the book of Amos for over a decade in both English and Hebrew, but not really understanding it until she approached it "from a place… acquainted with injustice."

While ministering in Stateville Prison, Van Opstal recounted how she "began to see Amos very differently" based on insights from the inmates she worked with. Amos "was a care-giver" who preached against "trampling on the poor, purchasing from companies that exploit workers… and cause war for our luxurious jewels and our electronic batteries." He also taught "that investing our wealth in funds that profit our retirement at the expense of incarcerated men and women and children in detention is not worship." After receiving an ovation from the crowd, Van Opstal proceeded to prosecute the church for "complicity in racist structures."[2]

She encouraged Cru staff to train "Christian activists" to fight against

---

1. Formerly "Campus Crusade for Christ."

2. Sandra Van Opstal, "General Session" (Cru19, Colorado State University, July 20, 2019), 1:05:25, 1:12:21.

things like "inequity in housing" and "white supremacy." In so doing, Christians would cease to be a "stench" to God and prove the legitimacy of their faith. In Van Opstal's mind, "speaking truth to power" was participating in the "revolution against evil and injustice" Jesus started which was "what the Gospel [was] about."[3]

While Amos did speak about justice, Van Opstal envisioned an interpretation of both the term and its application which closely paralleled the assumptions of modern secular progressives.

Though she never mentioned abortion, she did characterize deportations connected with border security as "another holocaust."[4] One could imagine much of her talk receiving a warm welcome at a political rally for a Democrat candidate. Yet, her speech was meant to be a lesson from the book of Amos.

What made Van Opstal's analysis different from historical interpretations, which focused more on personal sins, was the way she used an oppressed lens to derive meaning from the text. Insights from prisoners justified both her interpretation and application by revealing knowledge previously hidden from her despite extensive research and study. Her assumption, that oppression produced superior knowledge, is common among social justice activists.

Social Justice Gnostics

The eminent church historian Philip Schaff, described ancient Gnostic heresies as "attempt[s] to unfold mysteries of an upper world" while "disdain[ing] the trammels of reason, and resort[ing] to direct spiritual intuition." He wrote that "the highest source of knowledge, with these heretics, was a secret tradition." The goal of Gnostics was to escape the physical world of sense perception and reach a higher "ideal world."[5] Today's social justice movement shares a similar epistemology, or theory of truth, with ancient Gnosticism. However, instead of using secret traditions, social justice advocates seek knowledge through the perspectives of oppressed social locations in order to understand reality and escape oppression.

Patricia Hill Collins published *Black Feminist Thought* in 1990 in

3. Ibid., 1:13:25, 1:12:21, 1:19:35, 1:16:30.

4. Ibid., 1:20:50.

5. Philip Schaff, *History of the Christian Church,* vol. 2 (New York: Charles Scribner's Sons, 1901), 450-451, 455.

which she conceived of a world in which a complex "matrix of domination" oppressed certain social identities. In this reality, dominant groups favored unbiased tools of analysis such as "science," "reason" and "facts" in discovering truth and used their own standards to define other groups in negative ways. In order to accomplish "social justice," oppressed groups needed to reject these standards and consider their own understandings to be valid and valuable instead. Collins argued that unique "epistemological approaches" derived from different ethnic, gender, and sexual oriented "standpoints" could validate the truthfulness of ideas thus becoming "the most 'objective' truths."[6]

Feminist and postcolonial theorist Sandra Harding attributed this standpoint epistemology to "Marxian thought" imported into the "feminist critical theory" of the 1970s and 1980s. The underlying assumption was that different experiences produced different kinds of knowledge which in turn produced different understandings of reality. Standpoint theorists considered oppressed experiences to be superior understandings because they required knowing the standards of the group oppressing them as well as their own standards.[7] Voddie Baucham, a popular critic, refers to this thinking as "Ethnic Gnosticism" when applied to ethnic groups because it promotes "the idea that people have special knowledge based solely on their ethnicity."[8]

A belief in some version of standpoint epistemology is one of the most commonly shared traits linking social justice advocates across various concentrations. The Me Too, Black Lives Matter, anti-nationalist, gun control, and LGBTQIA+ normalization movements all promote emotional stories of victimhood to support the movement's core message while enjoying the benefit of unquestioned authority by nature of the victim's oppressed standpoint. The political advantage in harnessing oppressed perspectives, instead of appealing to science, logic, and evidence, is that most people think it impolite to contradict a personal story. This means social justice advocates can circumvent reasonable debate while shaming their opposition for alleged personal prejudice. Disagreement over a political position can be character-

6. Patricia Hill *Collins, Black Feminist Thought: Knowledge, Consciousness, and the Politics of Empowerment* (Unwin Hyman, 1990), 226, 256, 70, 196-197, xi, 256.

7. Sandra Harding, ed., *The Feminist Standpoint Theory Reader: Intellectual and Political Controversies*, 1st ed. (New York: Routledge, 2004), 1-3, 7, 162-163.

8. Baucham, *Fault Lines*, 92.

ized as motivated by racism, misogyny, nationalism, homophobia, or another vilifying pejorative.

After the 2018 mass shooting at Stoneman Douglas High School in Parkland, Florida, one of the survivors, an eighteen-year-old named David Hogg, became a national spokesman for gun control. Within two months, Hogg spoke at the March for Our Lives rally, appeared on the cover of *Time* magazine, and performed multiple television interviews in which he weighed in on questions of public policy. His only experience related to the subject was the fact that he survived a school shooting. Hogg accused those who disagreed with his positions, like Senator Marco Rubio and the National Rifle Association, of valuing money over the lives of children.[9]

Later that year, President Trump nominated a more conservative judge, Brett Kavanaugh, to replace retiring Supreme Court Justice Anthony Kennedy. During confirmation hearings, Christine Blasey Ford publicly charged Kavanaugh with attempting to rape her at a summer party in the 1980s which he denied. As a result, senators Kamala Harris and Kirsten Gillibrand posted #BelieveSurvivors on social media and a dating app called Bumble published a full-page ad in *The New York Times* with large white letters reading "Believe Women."[10] Ford also received approximately one million dollars from crowd funding efforts, several offers for book deals, and awards from the ACLU and YWCA Silicon Valley for bravery.[11] Despite lacking both hard and circumstantial evidence, many supporters characterized those who doubted her story as "misogynistic" or "sexist."[12]

---

9. David Hogg, *CNN: New Day*, interview by Alisyn Camerota, March 26, 2018.

10. Reagan McCarthy, "'Believing Women:' Harris and Gillibrand's New Campaign," *Townhall*, September 24, 2018, https://townhall.com/tipsheet/reaganmccarthy/2018/09/24/harris-and-gillibrands-hypocrisy-on-believing-women-n2522175; Morgan Gstalter, "Dating App Bumble Publishes Full-Page Ad in NY Times: 'Believe Women,'" *The Hill*, September 28, 2018. https://thehill.com/blogs/blog-briefing-room/news/408946-female-driven-dating-app-bumble-publishes-full-page-ad-in-the.

11. Katherine Rodriguez, "Christine Blasey Ford Rakes in $1 Million, Several Book Offers," *Breitbart*, October 29, 2018, https://www.breitbart.com/politics/2018/10/29/kavanaugh-accuser-christine-blasey-ford-rakes-in-1-million-several-book-offers/.

12. Jennifer Rubin, [@JRubinBlogger], 2018, "We don't yet have enough evidence to say definitively whether Kavanaugh attacked Christine Blasey Ford. By contrast, we have evidence beyond a reasonable doubt that President Trump's Republican Party has adopted misogyny as an election strategy.," Sept 25, 2018, 4:46 p.m., https://twitter.com/JRubinBlogger/status/1044689526663401474; Carolyn Maloney, [@RepMaloney], 2018,

Another example of social justice advocates appealing to subjective lived experience, instead of objective universal truths, concerns the controversy over transgender athletes. In 2019, biological males Terry Miller and Andraya Yearwood won first and second places in the State of Connecticut's 55-meter dash indoor track championships for high school females. Selina Soule, a biological female who came in third place, became part of a lawsuit challenging Connecticut's policy as discriminatory because it allowed boys to displace girls in track competitions. Instead of addressing Soule's argument, multiple people online called her "transphobic" and journalist Claire Goforth referred to her as the "darling of transphobes everywhere."[13]

In each case, voices promoting the standpoint of their allegedly oppressed social group enjoyed special protection from scrutiny and conclusions derived from their experience were beyond the realm of reason and debate. Curiously, Kyle Kashuv (who was also a survivor of the Parkland Shooting but supported gun rights), Tara Reade (who accused Democrat Joe Biden of sexual assault), and various Log Cabin Republican groups (that represent self-identifying transgender people but also oppose biological males competing against biological females) do not receive the same treatment. The reason for this is that only certain victims are qualified to represent their group's standpoint.

Standpoint Theory

Sandra Harding believed "empowerment" required knowledge that could "emerge only through a political process." A standpoint was not simply a "perspective," but rather, a kind of knowledge about hidden oppression that oppressed groups struggled to reveal. Only victims who were politically engaged against "dominant society" were capable of ascertaining this kind of secret knowledge.[14] For example, people like Clarence Thomas, Thomas Sowell, and Candace Owens did not qualify as representatives of black per-

---

"The Senate Judiciary Committee MUST do better by Christine Blasey Ford than it did by Anita Hill. Our society has come too far to allow its governing bodies to be ruled by sexism and misogyny. #MeToo," Sept 18, 2018, 11:49 a.m., https://twitter.com/RepMaloney/status/1042078235402690561.

13. Claire Goforth, "TikToker Roasts Transphobic Activist's Unsettling Tucker Carlson Appearance," *The Daily Dot*, February 12, 2021, https://www.dailydot.com/debug/transhobic-activist-tucker-carlson-selina-soule/.

14. Harding, *The Feminist Standpoint Reader*, 7-8.

spectives because of their political conservatism, despite their biological and cultural backgrounds. However, activists like James Cone, Al Sharpton, and Ibram X. Kendi did.

A simple way to conceive of this standpoint epistemology is to imagine a two-dimensional world comprised of red people, who represent the oppressed, and blue people who represent the oppressors. Both red and blue people live inside their respective red and blue boxes and see the world through the lens of their red and blue glasses. From the perspective of a red person, reality is a shade of red. From the perspective of a blue person, reality is a shade of blue. Standpoint theorists represent a third perspective that is able to transcend color, box, and lens in order to adjudicate between red and blue realities. They decree reality to be red and teach blue people to wear red glasses while staying silent about their blue opinions. Conversely, red people who wear blue glasses and hold blue opinions do not represent red people. However, the idea that a multicolored view exists contradicts the notion that all perspectives are classified according to red or blue social locations.

Feminist author Linda LeMoncheck pointed out the problem when she stated that by regarding certain perspectives as "prejudiced," postmodernists required "an impossible omniscience." Standpoint theorists needed to somehow step outside their own social location, understand and compare competing "versions of truth," and then determine which one was valid. Not only was this impossible for humans whose knowledge was supposed to be the product of their own narrow social group, but it produced a procedure for finding truth which was at least as demanding as the scientific process attributed to European males.[15]

Members of oppressed groups themselves were only capable of partial truth and knowledge. Even Patricia Hill Collins admitted that her own scholarship was determined, in part, by her social location and contained "subjective" elements.[16] Unfortunately, without the ability to escape one's own limited perspective in order to find universal principles that apply to all perspectives, there is no way to justify certainty about anything in an objective sense. If standpoint theorists are correct, no one is capable of making truth claims about anything outside of their narrow experiences,

15. Linda LeMoncheck, *Loose Women, Lecherous Men: A Feminist Philosophy of Sex* (Oxford University Press, 1997), 19; Collins, 203.

16. Ibid., xiv.

which means that no one is capable of making absolute truth claims at all. Despite this problem, standpoint theorists continue to act as if objective truth exists within their conception of oppressed standpoints though they cannot justify this idea without appealing to universal principles and undercutting their entire theory.

Woke Hermeneutics

As a result of their rhetorical success, the meanings of an ever-expanding list of concepts, symbols, items, literature, etc. now depend on interpretations derived from various oppressed social locations. Without a politically active minority lens, humans cannot clearly understand many facets of reality, including the meaning of divine revelation. Sandra Van Opstal is not the only leader in evangelical institutions to express this insecurity regarding biblical interpretation. Danny Akin, the president of Southeastern Baptist Theological Seminary, conveys a similar view.

In 2018, the Ethics and Religious Liberty Commission featured Akin in a video that asked the question, "What do white Christians need to be mindful of when speaking out about racial reconciliation?" Akin answered that "white Christians need to learn above all things... to be good listeners." The reason, he explained, was because the white perspective was "not the perspective of" African Americans, Hispanics, or Asians who saw "life differently" and operated "out of a different paradigm" and "context." In classic social justice fashion, Akin used this standpoint epistemology to argue that white people needed to "surrender leadership" to "ethnic minorities" in order to "make progress" toward racial equality.[17]

The next year, Akin encouraged his followers on social media to read an article from *Christianity Today* called "Black and Evangelical: Why I Keep the Label," which he described as "superb" because it both convicted and captured his heart.[18] One of the author's main goals was to explain the

---

17. Danny Akin, *What Do White Christians Need to Be Mindful of When Speaking out about Racial Reconciliation?* (Ethics and Religious Liberty Commission, 2018), https://vimeo.com/263621124.

18. Daniel Akin, [@DannyAkin], 2019, "Black and Evangelical: Why I Keep the Label | Christianity Today/ A superb article that so well convicts and captures my heart all at once. Please give it a few moments. You will be glad you did. https://christianitytoday.com/

differences between white and black evangelicals. It said, "personal and cultural experiences create lenses that are essential to the discovery of objective truths." Not surprisingly, the author did not believe all cultural experiences were equal. He wrote that George Whitefield's "racism… prompted the experiential formation of [an] African American theological method" that "allowed them to see the objective truth."[19]

In 2020, Akin again encouraged a form of standpoint epistemology. In an interview at Southeastern, he said it was "better" to "read the Bible" with people "from all different ethnicities" and "socioeconomic standings because they're going to have insights" into the Bible that he would miss.[20] Both critical theory expert James Lindsay and Christian apologist Bill Roach recognized Akin's statements paralleled the subjectivity found in critical race theory.[21] Though, Neil Shenvi, a popular Christian blogger and former chemist, defended Akin by appealing, in part, to a rationale commonly invoked in order to justify claims made by critical race theorists.

Shenvi argued that "simply saying 'we all have blind spots and we'll be better able to recognize them if we talk to each other' [wasn't] standpoint epistemology," especially since Akin also believed in the authority of Scripture.[22] However, the problem with statements like Akin's is not the

---

ct/2019/march-web-only/black-and-evangelical-why-i-keep-label.html" Mar 30, 2019, 7:39 a.m., https://twitter.com/DannyAkin/status/1111956073676787713.

19. Brandon Washington, "Black and Evangelical: Why I Keep the Label," *Christianity Today*, March 28, 2019, https://www.christianitytoday.com/ct/2019/march-web-only/black-and-evangelical-why-i-keep-label.html.

20. Danny Akin, *SBC Q&A With Danny Akin* (Wake Forest, NC: Southeastern Baptist Theological Seminary, 2020), 30:40, https://youtu.be/7uyCAz4hS0s.

21. James Lindsay, [@ConceptualJames], 2020, "This is the spawn of standpoint epistemology (a radical feminist idea) as it mated with critical race Theory's interpretation of Foucault's postmodern ideas about how dominant discourses and various contingencies shape truth, mixed with biblical inerrancy. LOL. Yikes.," April 9, 2020, 10:28 a.m., https://twitter.com/ConceptualJames/status/1248256413996064772; Bill Roach, [@billroach_], 2020, "The issue is not about influence. Rather the issue is whether or not one can ontologically overcome their particular horizon. CRT, I, and so forth, due to their metaphysic, deny this is even possible. But, accordjng to this view, even,if you are aware, you can't shake them.," April 9, 2020, 7:02 p.m., https://twitter.com/billroach_/status/1248385708105953287.

22. Neil Shenvi, [@NeilShenvi], 2020, "IOW, simply saying "we all have blind spots and we'll be better able to recognize them if we talk to each other" isn't standpoint epistemology (at least in Harding's sense). Especially if you add: "My theology is correct and black

admission that people can learn from one another, but rather the assumption that social location determines understanding.

For example, Akin's logic would not, at least yet, be applied to a brain surgery scenario. The metric currently used to certify a doctor's competency is related to expertise and ability, not social location. While someone from a culture that values education may find concepts related to brain surgery easier to grasp, their authority on the subject is wholly related to their real-world achievement, not their cultural or ethnic background. Furthermore, brain surgeons do not evaluate the legitimacy of their methods by submitting them to a panel of ethnically diverse surgeons for approval. Instead, they use objective analysis, regardless of their ethnicity, in order to pursue a successful outcome. This is the basic standard desired and expected of doctors but not, unfortunately, of Bible interpreters.

In a panel discussion later that year, Akin again reiterated: "Theology is the best in community and not only in community of white culture, but in community of diverse cultures and diverse ethnicities because we all bring insights to the same inspired text that the others miss. And that's just simply a reality in terms of race, in terms of gender, [and] in terms of socioeconomic standing."[23] Individuals who make such absolute claims concerning the priority of diverse ethnic interpretations often fail to realize that if their view were true, it also would be the result of their own limited and inadequate social location. Not only is this logic self-defeating, but it is also contrary to the way Scripture envisions interpretation.

Though the Spirit of God enlightens the minds of believers as they read the Bible, the truth contained therein is rationally accessible regardless of one's social location.[24] The Apostle Paul believed it was the "diligent… workman" who "accurately handl[ed] the word of truth" and "the man of God" to whom "all Scripture" was made "profitable."[25] If separation existed between different people's ability to interpret revelation, it related to whether

---

lesbians should accept it"," April 9, 2020, 6:32 p.m., https://twitter.com/NeilShenvi/status/1248378180894781440.

23. Danny Akin, *A Conversation Regarding Theology, Ethics, and Racial Injustice* (Wake Forest, NC: Southeastern Baptist Theological Seminary, 2020), 34:40, https://youtu.be/cFsOZhu_E_s.

24. Matt 13:11; John 14:26; 16:13-16; 1 Cor 2:10, 14

25. 2 Tim 2:15; 3:16-17

or not they studied, listened, and learned. Throughout the Bible, there are numerous examples of people learning from others based upon their wisdom, virtue, and authority.[26] Yet, lived experience resulting from social location is never presented as the basis for any of these qualities.

If people first need to possess knowledge exclusively based on external factors, such as nationality and gender, in order to understand God's world and word, revelation is no longer clear and efficient. The Apostle Paul could not have told the pagan philosophers on Mars Hill that God made "every nation of mankind" to "seek," "grope for," and "find" Him, or that "all people everywhere should repent," or that the resurrection of Christ was "proof to all men" of coming judgement.[27] Neither could he say to the Christians in Rome that even unredeemed men were equipped with the knowledge, evidence, apprehension, and understanding of God's "eternal power and divine nature."[28] Postmodern standpoint epistemology destroys this Christian conception of revelation's accessibility by placing knowledge barriers in front of people from certain social locations. And, like most false teachings, Christians have answered the errors associated with today's social justice subjectivity once before.

Attacking Truth

The understanding of truth that much of the mainstream academia and media operate by is consistent with 20th century philosopher Hans-Georg Gadamer's "horizons" view. Gadamer taught that meaning was found through a fusion of experience between the reader and listener. Neo-evangelical thinker Carl F. H. Henry described Gadamer's approach as a "new hermeneutic" because it regarded the "interpreter as the source of meaning itself, rather than merely an agent of interpretation and translation." Henry believed Gadamer's claims made "cultural differences between eras... so radical and absolute that even the most painstaking historical study [could not] recapture the meaning of the past documents."[29] Thus, the horizons

---

26. Prov 1:5; 5:1, 6:20; Phil 4:9; 1 Cor 4:6-16; 11:1; 1 Tim 2:11

27. Acts 17:26-31

28. Rom 1:19-20

29. Carl F. H. Henry, God, *Revelation and Authority: God Who Speaks and Shows*, vol. 4

view threatened the ability of modern Americans, for example, to understand ancient books like the Bible.

Christian apologist Norm Geisler also saw the horizon's view as a problem because it made the meaning of a text subject to a reader's understanding and application. While Scripture's meaning should be applied to a reader's life, Geisler believed a reader's "understanding [had] no hermeneutically definitive role" and "specific application should not color the interpretation of a passage."[30] In 1982, Henry and Geisler, along with other famous theologians such as R. C. Sproul, James Montgomery Boice, and John MacArthur adopted the Chicago Statement on Biblical Hermeneutics. In the document they denied "that the 'horizons' of the biblical writer and the interpreter may rightly 'fuse' in such a way that what the text communicates to the interpreter is not ultimately controlled by the expressed meaning of the Scripture."[31]

In his book *Defending Evangelicalism: The Apologetics of Norman L. Geisler*, Christian apologist Bill Roach applied Geisler's thinking to today's subjectivity motivated by social justice. He wrote that in the Bible "religious disagreements were not the mere product of different cultures, standpoint epistemologies, or perspective." Instead, Scripture provided answers to false ideas and never "chang[ed] the attributes of God or alter[ed] the total truthfulness of Scripture unto pagan ideas or culturally accepted Greco-Roman academic standards."[32] Unlike the men who crafted the *Chicago Statement*, many modern evangelicals think its advantageous to conform Christian teaching and ministry to the standards created by standpoint theorists motivated by social justice.

In 2017, The United Methodist Church hired Robin DiAngelo, the author of *White Fragility*, to lecture on "Deconstructing White Privilege." In her speech, DiAngelo credited "white supremacy" for her own "psycho-social development," "personality," and "worldview," while challenging white people's "implicit bias." According to DiAngelo, people of color pos-

(Crossway, 1999), 304, 463; Gregory Alan Thornbury, *Recovering Classic Evangelicalism: Applying the Wisdom and Vision of Carl F. H. Henry* (Crossway, 2013), 146.

30. Earl Radmacher and Robert Preus, eds., *Hermeneutics, Inerrancy, and the Bible* (Grand Rapids: Zondervan, 1984), 883.

31. Ibid., 885.

32. William Roach, *Defending Evangelicalism: The Apologetics of Norman L. Geisler* (Christian Publishing House, 2020), 159.

sessed a superior awareness of white people's "inevitable racism" due to their oppressed experiences.[33] The next year, Bethany Jenkins, a senior fellow at The King's College and contributor for The Gospel Coalition, suggested that people whose theology is shaped by white male Christian authors should "consider expanding [their] library." Popular Christian speaker Beth Moore agreed declaring that Christians were too "theologically shaped" by white authors and it was "past time" to diversify "personal libraries" that had "failed and robbed us." [34]

In 2019, Esau McCaulley, an assistant professor of New Testament at Wheaton College suggested that ethnic minorities and women should be involved in Bible translation simply because "all translation is interpretation and interpretation is influenced by social location."[35] In an opinion piece for the *Washington Post*, McCaulley wrote "that more diverse translation committees could inspire fresh confidence among Christians of color" by allowing "black Christians and others to 'know with certainty the things that you have been taught' (Luke 1:4)."[36] Danny Carroll, another Wheaton College professor, has promoted the idea that Hispanics can "engage the text [of Scripture] at levels" others cannot simply because of their immigration experiences.[37] In a 2019 lecture at Charlotte's Gordon-Conwell seminary campus, Carroll taught that "the Bible takes a very different spin" for Hispanics who learn to see themselves in the text of Scripture "in ways a majority

33. Robin DiAngelo, "Deconstructing White Privilege with Dr. Robin DiAngelo," YouTube Video, 2017, https://www.youtube.com/watch?v=DwIx3KQer54&t=752s.

34. Beth Moore, [@BethMooreLPM], 2018, "So agree. It's way past time to inventory our personal libraries, to add to them where they are woefully lacking & to quit being clay theologically shaped by only one shade of hands. That needs to be over. It has failed and robbed us. For starters, Jesus didn't have white hands.," November 21, 2018, 7:56 a.m., https://twitter.com/BethMooreLPM/status/1065227573586735104

35. Esau McCaulley, [@esaumccaulley], 2019, "A question that I can't stop asking: If all translation is interpretation and interpretation is influenced by social location, what does it mean that most of our English bibles were translated with very few Black or other Christians of color or women involved?," September 8, 2019, 7:59 a.m., http://web.archive.org/web/20190908150157if_/https://twitter.com/esaumccaulley/status/1170713283243970560

36. Esau McCaulley, "Why It Matters If Your Bible Was Translated by a Racially Diverse Group," *The Washington Post*, September 23, 2019, https://www.washingtonpost.com/religion/2019/09/23/why-it-matters-if-your-bible-was-translated-by-a-racially-diverse-group/.

37. Danny Carroll, "Migration in the Bible: Entering the Stories, Expanding Our Vision - Danny Carroll," YouTube Video, Dallas Theological Seminary, November 7, 2013, 4:00 https://www.youtube.com/watch?v=JkEoRLfIUSM.

culture person cannot understand."[38] Standpoint epistemology is impacting the way evangelicals think about ethics, theology, academics, and politics. In the Southern Baptist Convention, the "Caring Well Initiative" applies a mild version of standpoint epistemology to the issue of sexual abuse.

According to then president of the convention J. D. Greear, the purpose of the Caring Well Initiative was to help churches engage the problem of abuse.[39] However, many of the speakers for the training material had little to qualify them except for the fact that they experienced abuse. Even contributors who did possess expertise "took a posture of saying let's hear from [victim's] experience" before sharing their knowledge.[40] Of the twenty main speakers providing training, only four were publicly verifiable members of the clergy and only one, a counseling pastor from J. D. Greear's church, spoke in his capacity as a pastor. Greear taught that if church leaders were not first to rush to defend abuse survivors, they were "betray[ing] the name of Christ" and the gospel.[41]

The Caring Well Initiative, which did not platform male victims in their main teachings, mirrored the kind of thinking behind the Me Too movement's "believe women" slogan. Women who experienced sexual abuse were more qualified to advise pastors and churches on the topic of sexual abuse than were pastors who rightly understood and applied Scripture's teaching on the subject. Not only was their voice necessary for solving sexual abuse, but their stories were generally accepted without affirming the importance of verification. In the book *Becoming a Church That Cares Well for the Abused*, Caring Well contributors provided additional training in which they emphasized the importance of believing victims.

The book instructed pastors and ministry leaders to emphasize their belief in the victim's story and create a "safe space" where the victim felt believed. Leaders were to disregard "innocence until proven guilty," since it

38. Danny Carroll, "What the Bible Has To Say About Immigration; Dr. Daniel Carroll," YouTube Video, Gordon-Conwell Charlotte, September 9, 2019, https://www.youtube.com/watch?v=VFQ2m9BKWPM.

39. "Caring Well Initiative," https://caringwell.com/, accessed June 3, 2021, https://caringwell.com/.

40. *Panel: Sexual Abuse in the Southern Baptist Convention*, Caring Well Conference, 2019, 2:20, https://vimeo.com/365106400.

41. J. D. Greear, "Overturning Myths Related to Sexual Abuse and the Church - J.D. Greear," 1:00, https://vimeo.com/365105474.

only applied in the legal realm, while instead practicing Paul's teaching in 1 Corinthians 13:7 that "love believes all things." According to the book, a victim may suffer more trauma from not being believed than from their actual abuse.[42] This made reflexively believing victims a top priority.

However, in the context of 1 Corinthians 13:7, Paul was correcting the way Corinthian Christians pridefully misused their spiritual gifts by contrasting their arrogant attitudes with a spirit of love. Paul did not teach that victims had the right to be believed simply because of their stated experience or gender. Instead, he described the kind of encouraging attitude Christians should have toward each other in using their spiritual gifts. As Puritan Theologian Matthew Henry stated, "charity does by no means destroy prudence."[43] Paul himself did not immediately believe every detail of an accusation just because it was made.[44] Other passages warn against believing everything one is told without consideration in the civil, ecclesiastical, and personal realms.[45] Love does not compel someone to immediately believe a story simply because it came from someone claiming a victim experience. As 1 Corinthians 7:6 states, "[Love] rejoices with the truth." Yet, under siege today is the very concept of truth itself.

Pragmatic Pulpits

In the 1993 book *No Place For Truth*, theologian David Well's observed that Christians increasingly found themselves living in a "pragmatic world... hostile to absolute principles and transcendent meaning" which saw "truth as whatever works." As a result, evangelicals increasingly abandoned theological practice in favor of a "pragmatic rationale" centered on "needs." Well's wrote that the Church's "fidelity came to be measured by activities it arranged" that "had less and less to do with love of God and more and more to do with the love of neighbor until in the end the one was subsumed under the other."

---

42. Brad Hambrick, ed., *Becoming a Church That Cares Well for the Abused: Handbook* (Nashville, TN: B&H Publishing, 2019), 67-41, 87, 20.

43. Matthew Henry, "Commentary on 1 Corinthians 13," Blue Letter Bible, accessed June 3, 2021, https://www.blueletterbible.org/Comm/mhc/1Cr/1Cr_013.cfm.

44. 1 Cor 11:18

45. Deut 19:15; Matt 18:16; 1 Tim 5:19; Prov 14:15

Eventually, "faith came to mean little more than seeking justice in the world" and "social justice... was listed as a pastoral priority."[46]

While some evangelicals truly believe in standpoint epistemology, there are also many who adopt applications of it for pragmatic reasons. For example, Rebecca McLaughlin, an author and contributor for The Gospel Coalition, asserted that "in an age where who you are determines what you have the right to say, we also need to stop fielding straight white men."[47] Evangelical author and speaker Skye Jethani stated the church needed minority leaders, as opposed to white leaders, because they "have a perspective and a skill set that is needed in our pluralistic moment that a lot of white leaders just, frankly, don't have."[48] The Send Institute, which partners with Wheaton College and the Southern Baptist Convention, called for a "diverse and globally-minded mission force" to replace "prevalent church planting models" in order to respond to "increasing racial and ethnic diversity," religious pluralism, and secularism.[49] Such statements beg the question as to whether or not ethnically diverse perspectives would be needed if cultural circumstances were different.

Whether proponents of modern standpoint theory are acting on pragmatism or truly believe experiences formed from disadvantaged social locations produce greater insights into reality, they are certainly promoting a kind of subjectivity incompatible with Christian epistemology. As this thinking becomes more entrenched and finds applications that override Christian ethics, the conflict between modern social justice and Christianity becomes more obvious.

At Tuskegee University's 2020 Dr. Martin Luther King Jr. Convocation, Rev. Dr. Raphael Warnock gave a glimpse of what lies ahead for evangelicals if they continue down the path of social justice subjectivity. Warnock, who

46. David Wells, *No Place for Truth: Or Whatever Happened to Evangelical Theology?* (Wm. B. Eerdmans Publishing, 1994), 112, 126, 243, 254, 233.

47. Rebecca McLaughlin, *What We Need to Confront About Christianity*, interview by Collin Hansen, March 19, 2019, https://www.thegospelcoalition.org/podcasts/tgc-podcast/need-confront-christianity/.

48. Phil Vischer, "Episode 433: Ending the War on Drugs with Bonnie Kristian - The Holy Post," accessed June 7, 2021, 35:30, https://podcast.app/ending-the-war-on-drugs-with-bonnie-kristian-e123339876/.

49. Ed Stetzer et al., "A Church Planting Manifesto for 21 Century North America," Send Institute, accessed June 8, 2021, https://www.sendinstitute.org/manifesto/.

was mentored by liberation theologian James Cone, made the case that men, white people, and the able-bodied, needed the perspectives of women, black people, and the disabled in order to understand "God's glory." Then, he went a step further. Warnock declared: "I hear our LGBTQ sisters and brothers standing up saying to those of us who are straight and heterosexual, that you don't know what it's like to live in my body, to have my experience… . before you shut them down, recognize that there are some things you can only see from certain perspectives."[50] The faint murmurs of Warnock's logic are already whispered in certain quarters of evangelicalism by organizations such as Revoice and Living Out.[51]

Christian Realism

If Christians are to retain the authority of Scripture, biblical ethics, and the mission of the church, they will need to reject social justice subjectivity and return to an objective understanding of reality. This does not mean a return to the Enlightenment, which generally "aimed at accounting for the whole of life strictly from within the bounds of natural reason."[52] Nor does it require adopting a version of empiricism or rationalism, both of which only provide an illusory objectivity that quickly collapses into subjectivity by making man the measure of all things.

Instead, Christians must recapture a kind of realism exemplified in both the biblical text and their own tradition. Philosopher Paul Tyson wrote that Christians needed to "return to a vision of reality that is grounded in revealed truth of a genuinely spiritual and transcendently sourced nature."[53] In other words, God gave humans tools like sense perception, a conscience,

50. Raphael Warnock, *2020 Dr. Martin Luther King Jr. Annual Convocation*, YouTube Video, Tuskegee University, 2020, 51:00, https://www.youtube.com/watch?v=0egqeZD7R-g&t=0s.

51. Preston Sprinkle, "5 Things Every Christian Should Know about the Transgender Conversation," Living Out, June 8, 2021, https://www.livingout.org/resources/articles/83/5-things-every-christian-should-know-about-the-transgender-conversation; Revoice19 - Mark Yarhouse - General Session 3, YouTube Video, Revoice Conference, 2019, https://www.youtube.com/watch?v=6XsAKp1N2uc.

52. Wells, *No Place For Truth*, 57-60.

53. Paul Tyson, *Returning to Reality: Christian Platonism for Our Times* (Wipf and Stock Publishers, 2014), 210.

and reason. He also imparted special revelation through the ministry of the Holy Spirit who "convict[s] the world," teaches believers, and inspired men to write Scripture.[54] Yet, this access into reality is not grounded in finite humans themselves, but rather an invariable, absolute, and unchanging God. Without the transcendence of an eternal realm, there can be no real meaning in the temporal.

Tyson warned that "without such vision, we will only have amoral power, instrumental exploitation, and a deepening blindness to the actual human truths that give meaning and purpose to our existence."[55] Unfortunately, this is the path social justice advocates have chosen. Instead of grounding truth in the divine and universal, they prefer to do it in particular created beings. They believe some people possess the ability to know things, while others do not, by nature of temporal conditions like social location and political involvement. Christians should know better. The Creator still speaks through revelation in such a way people can know both Him and the world He made for them to dwell in.

---

54. John 16:8; 14:26; 2 Pet 1:21

55. Tyson, *Returning to Reality*, 210.

CHAPTER 5
SOCIAL JUSTICE METAPHYSICS

AT THE JANUARY 2019 March for Life, *The Washington Post* and CNN used a short video clip to falsely report that Nicholas Sandmann, a student with the Covington Catholic High School, confronted Nathan Phillips, a Native American activist, by walking up to him and smirking while wearing a MAGA hat. Immediately, an avalanche of strong condemnations ensued, many of them later retracted or deleted when the story proved to be false.

The Secretary of State of Kentucky lashed out against adults who taught and allowed students to defy Kentucky values by enacting such "horrific scenes."[1] Comedian and actress Kathy Griffin called for doxing and shaming the teenagers.[2] Even Covington Catholic High School and the Diocese of Covington "condemn[ed] the actions" of the students "toward Nathan Phillips" claiming they were "opposed to the Church's teachings on the dignity and respect of the human person."[3] Film producer Jack Morrissey went so far as to post an image of "MAGAkids go[ing] screaming, hats first, into the

---

1. Alison Grimes, Facebook, January 19, 2019, https:// www.facebook.com/ junotdiaz. writer/ posts/ 972495572815454.

2. Tyler McCarthy, "Kathy Griffin Calls for Doxing Student's Identities after Viral Video at Native American March: 'Shame Them,'" *Fox News,* January 21, 2019, https://www.foxnews. com/entertainment/kathy-griffin-calls-for-doxing-students-in-viral-video-shame-them.

3. Max Londberg, "'Blatant Racism': Ky. High School Apologizes Following Backlash after Video Shows Students Surrounding Indigenous Marchers," *USA Today,* January 24, 2019, https://www.usatoday.com/story/news/nation/2019/01/19/kentucky-diocese-incident-indigenous-peoples-march-covington-catholic-high-school/2624503002/.

woodchipper."[4] Unfortunately, progressive-leaning voices in the evangelical world also reflexively took part in denouncing the students.

Thabiti Anyawbile, an author and pastor affiliated with 9Marks ministries at the time, encouraged "vigilant" opposition to the "racist incivility" promoted by "some professing Christians."[5] Karen Swallow Prior, a popular Christian author and current professor at Southeastern Baptist Theological Seminary, said she was "sick to [her] stomach." Then president of the Southern Baptist Convention J. D. Greear, agreed that Sandmann displayed "hate."[6] Duke Kwon, a pastor and author associated with the Presbyterian Church in America, attacked the "pro-life Movement" for making it "difficult for Christians of color to participate."[7]

Perhaps the strongest denunciation came from Beth Moore who stated: "To glee in dehumanizing any person is so utterly antichrist it reeks of the vomit of hell." She followed up her Tweet with another in which she declared: "I cannot shake the terror of adolescents already indoctrinated enough in hate and disrespect to smile that chillingly and jeer without shame or fear of God. Uncurbed, this utter glee in dehumanizing is what humanitarian horrors are made of."[8]

Two days after the incident, an unedited video revealed that it was in

---

4. Levine Jon and Hod Itay, "Jack Morrissey Apologizes for Deleted Covington 'Woodchipper' Tweet," *The Wrap* (blog), January 22, 2019, https://www.thewrap.com/film-producer-jack-morrissey-apologizes-for-deleted-covington-woodchipper-tweet/.

5. Thabiti Anyabwile [@ThabitiAnyabwil], 2019, "This is the kind of racist incivility that now has some measure of acceptance in our streets and our highest offices. That it also appears at Christian events and comes from some professing Christians makes it 1000 times worse. We have to be vigilant in opposing this stuff.," Jan 19, 2019, 9:44 a.m., https://twitter.com/ThabitiAnyabwil/status/108663548988357427.

6. Stephen Wolfe, "The Covington Kids and Evangelical Elite Mobbery," *Sovereign Nations* (blog), January 23, 2019, https://sovereignnations.com/2019/01/23/covington-kids-evangelical-elite-mobbery/.

7. Duke Kwon [@dukekwondc], 2019, "The incident involving the boy(s) and Native American elder is disturbing but hardly surprising. In fact, it illustrates how the culture of the pro-life Movement and March for Life makes it difficult for Christians of color to participate even when their convictions are aligned.," Jan 19, 2019, 1:44 p.m., hhttps://twitter.com/dukekwondc/status/1086695798937714688.

8. Mary Beth Brown, "Mary Beth Brown: Beth Moore Is Using Marxist, Feminist, Social Justice Talking Points Instead of Scripture," *The Western Journal*, July 31, 2020, https://www.westernjournal.com/mary-beth-brown-beth-moore-using-marxist-feminist-social-justice-talking-points-instead-scripture/.

fact a group of Black Hebrew Israelites who directed racial slurs toward the teenagers and Nathan Philips was the one to actually confront Nicholas Sandmann, not the other way around. Media organizations, celebrities, and even religious leaders were guilty of rushing to judgment before knowing the full story, believing Phillip's testimony that he was trapped by the Covington students and Sandmann blocked his attempt to escape,. As a result, some of the evangelical leaders who took part in blaming Sandmann expressed frustration with their initial reaction, but none publicly apologized for slandering him. Fortunately for Sandmann, exonerating evidence appeared while the news cycle was still fresh. If it had not, it is likely the court of public opinion would have reached its verdict and moved on to other matters leaving Sandmann the victim of trial-by-media.

Distorting Reality

Unfortunately, media malpractice is considered quite common. A recent poll suggests that a little over half of Americans do not even trust the media and numbers are falling.[9] Instead of seeking to understand and describe events, many people believe political agendas drive today's news reports. Journalists, sociologists, and historians no longer try to form explanations that make sense of all the available evidence surrounding a situation. Instead, they subvert interpretive standards in order to advance an ideology, generally driven by social justice.

Recently, both the national and international media promoted the narrative that systemic racism permeated American policing while extensively covering the deaths of black individuals George Floyd and Brianna Taylor. Yet, they practically ignored the deaths of white individuals Tony Timpa and Duncan Lemp who died under similar circumstances.[10] Many traditional news outlets also emphasized the threat militias posed after Kyle Rittenhouse,

9. Raghavan Mayur, "Less Than Half Of All Americans Trust The Media, Traditional Or Alternative! What Can The Media Do To Restore Its Trust Factor?," *Tipp Insights*, May 21, 2021, https://tippinsights.com/less-than-half-of-all-americans-trust-the-media-traditional-or-new-what-can-the-media-do-to-restore-its-trust-factor/.

10. Ryan Mills, "Tony Timpa Suffered the Same Fate as George Floyd – But Received None of the Attention," *National Review*, May 6, 2021, https://www.nationalreview.com/news/tony-timpa-suffered-the-same-fate-as-george-floyd-but-received-none-of-the-attention/; C.J. Ciaramella, "Maryland Man Killed in No-Knock SWAT Raid Was Shot

a white teenager, fatally shot a black protestor man named Joseph Rosenbaum in alleged self-defense. However, when a black Capitol police officer fatally shot a white protestor named Ashli Babbitt in alleged self-defense two months later, there was hardly any concern over bias or incompetence on the part of Capitol police. Likewise, in early 2021, mainstream media outlets generally declined to report the ethnicities of black perpetrators who murdered Asian American victims such as Vichar Ratanapakdee, Pak Ho, and Mohammad Anwar. Nevertheless, when Robert Long murdered eight people at three massage parlors in Atlanta, six of whom were Asian, news organizations highlighted Long's white ethnicity, almost ignored his two white victims, and increased calls to challenge racism and white supremacy.

Behind this double standard in reporting exists a presupposed narrative governing the way media and academic elites approach their work. When interpreting a news story, historical event, or sociological survey, shapers of public opinion often consider how to frame a particular situation to advance their ideological and political objectives. News anchors Katy Tur and Jorge Ramos admitted this at a National Press Club panel in 2017 when both expressed commitments to unbiased journalism yet simultaneously imposed their own negative opinions about the election of President Donald Trump.

Tur stated that if journalists had any bias, it was a "bias towards the facts." Yet a few seconds later she accused Donald Trump of appealing to voters "most based fears," "frustrations," and "angers." Ramos asserted that the "first responsibility" of journalists was to "reflect reality." However, he also then described why journalists could not "remain neutral" toward someone like Donald Trump whom he characterized as a lying racist sexist xenophobic bully. The key to understanding Katy Tur's and Jorge Ramos's seemingly contradictory statements lies in their ideological objectives.

In addition to "an adherence to truth," Tur described the job of journalists as supporting the "principle" of "democracy." Similarly, Ramos said it was a journalist's job "to challenge and question those who are in power."[11] Both sentiments are rooted in a commitment to a certain kind of equality mani-

---

While Asleep, Family Says," *Reason*, March 16, 2020, https://reason.com/2020/03/16/maryland-man-killed-in-no-knock-swat-raid-was-shot-while-asleep-family-says/.

11. Jack Heretik, "Katy Tur Claims Journalists Aren't Biased As Jorge Ramos Rants Against Trump," *Washington Free Beacon*, April 28, 2017, https://freebeacon.com/politics/katy-tur-claims-journalists-arent-biased-jorge-ramos-lambasts-trump/.

fested politically in democracy and maintained by opposing those with the power to threaten it. Interestingly, neither seemed to realize that supporting democracy and challenging power are not necessary components for objectively reporting facts. By conflating their ideological goals with professional standards, both Tur and Ramos exposed their own bias and showed they were probably no different than the vast majority of journalists and academics.

A 2020 survey from the National Association of Scholars found that for every dollar college professors donated to a Republican cause, they donated twenty-one dollars to a Democrat cause.[12] Other studies confirm that traditional media and social media employees also give over 90% of their political donations to Democrat causes as opposed to Republican ones.[13] This means that a great portion of the most influential people in the country are politically motivated in one direction.

Because of the reputation their institutions have for high standards, they are able to effectively spread their ideological assumptions as if they were simply the products of neutral reason. Yet simultaneously they deny religion and tradition this status by relegating them to the realm of personal experience and uncertainty. This is how centers of information revolutionize society. Those still loyal to the Christian order that included a "clear moral and social hierarchy," "the existence of good and evil," and "the principle of sacrifice" are attacked and demonized as abusive, bigoted, and ignorant.[14] This is why, despite the pervasiveness of social justice, some impoverished and marginalized groups do not qualify for political defense or social assistance.

Consider for example a large demographic in the United States made up of twenty-five million people who experience great disparities when compared to the general population. They have higher poverty rates, lower

12. Mitchell Langbert and Sean Stevens, "Partisan Registration and Contributions of Faculty in Flagship Colleges by Sean Stevens," January 17, 2020, https://www.nas.org/blogs/article/partisan-registration-and-contributions-of-faculty-in-flagship-colleges.

13. Jennifer Smith, "90% of Facebook and Twitter Staff Donations Is to Democrats," *Daily Mail*, October 16, 2020, https://www.msn.com/en-us/news/politics/90percent-of-facebook-and-twitter-staff-donations-is-to-democrats/ar-BB1a6Hjh; Paul Bedard, "90% of Media Political Donations to Biden, Sanders, AOC, Democrats: Report," *Washington Examiner*, October 28, 2020, https://www.washingtonexaminer.com/washington-secrets/90-of-media-political-donations-to-biden-sanders-aoc-democrats-report.

14. Samuel Lively, *The Trojan Mouse: How Disney Is Winning the Culture War* (Sword of Goliath, 2019), loc 36–51. Kindle.

household incomes, and less access to healthcare. This likely contributes to their higher percentage of "obesity, smoking, and physical inactivity" cases. They also lead the country in infant mortalities as well as seven of the top ten causes of death, including drug overdoses.[15] During the last three decades, politicians persuaded many of them that building state and federal prisons would help answer their economic woes only to find instead they contributed to them by increasing poverty.[16]

It would be easy to trace a line of abuse toward them going back hundreds of years. The Union Army made total war against many of their ancestors; the government displaced more than five hundred of their families to form Shenandoah National Park; more recently, outsourcing and coal mining regulations contributed to massive job displacement; and stigmas surrounding some of their identifying characteristics, such as their appearance and accent, create opportunities for prejudice and discrimination.[17]

It would come as no surprise if someone reading the first paragraph describing these Appalachian Mountain dwellers concluded they represented a racial or religious minority. However, they are actually primarily Chris-

---

15. "Creating a Culture of Health in Appalachia" (Appalachian Regional Commission, August 2017).

16. Robert Todd Perdue and Kenneth Sanchagrin, "Imprisoning Appalachia: The Socio-Economic Impacts of Prison Development," *Journal of Appalachian Studies* 22, no. 2 (2016): 210–23, https://doi.org/10.5406/jappastud.22.2.0210.

17. John Heatwole, *The Burning: Sheridan in the Shenandoah Valley* (Rockbridge Pub., 1998); Audry Horning, "The Displaced - Shenandoah National Park (U.S. National Park Service)," National Park Service, February 26, 2015, https://www.nps.gov/shen/learn/historyculture/displaced.htm; "Appalachia and its workers proved less resilient in the face of displacement than other U.S. workers." See Stephen Herzenberg, Mark Price, and Wial Howard, "Displacement in Appalachia and the Non-Appalachian United States, 1993-2003: Findings Based on Five Displaced Worker Surveys" (Keystone Research Center, December 1, 2005); There is an over 76% decline since 1985 in coal mining jobs as of May 2021. See U.S. Bureau of Labor Statistics, "All Employees, Coal Mining," FRED, Federal Reserve Bank of St. Louis (FRED, Federal Reserve Bank of St. Louis, January 1, 1985), https://fred.stlouisfed.org/series/CES1021210001; Nicolas Loris, "The Many Problems of the EPA's Clean Power Plan and Climate Regulations: A Primer," The Heritage Foundation, July 7, 2015, https://www.heritage.org/environment/report/the-many-problems-the-epas-clean-power-plan-and-climate-regulations-primer; "For college students who speak stigmatized dialects such as Appalachian English, language can present some challenges that students who speak more standardized varieties are less likely to face." See Dunstan Stephany and Jaeger Audrey, "Dialect and Influences on the Academic Experiences of College Students," *The Journal of Higher Education* 86, no. 5 (October 2015).

tian and of Scotts-Irish stock. Though they would be prime candidates for social-justice-styled reparations, affirmative action, their own history month and many other compensatory campaigns, highlighting their mistreatment and poverty fails to serve the cause of the current social justice movement's negative posture toward Western Christianity and white privilege.[18]

In other words, the inhabitants of Appalachia vote conservatively and are still loyal to the old order, which is the very thing academics and journalists think holds back society's progression toward greater equality. Focusing on their affliction would also weaken narratives, such as "systemic racism," which are necessary in order to justify deconstructing and fundamentally reshaping society. In essence, the only acceptable victim narratives are those that can be used to further the current revolution. The recent focus on racial equity has been especially successful in this regard.

Assuming Oppression

Communists believed for a long time they could use racial disparities in the United States to further their own goals. In 1921, the Workers Party of America voiced their intention to "help [black people] in their fight for economic, political and social equality… and bind them into a solid union of revolutionary forces for the overthrow of our common enemy."[19] In 1958, Manning Johnson, a former leader for the National Committee of the Communist Party, described how Moscow targeted many black people, including pastors, to promote their agenda. They stirred up conflict and convinced many to blame white people in general and capitalism in particular for the injustices they experienced. As a result, Johnson wrote they effectively "wiped out" the "racial progress based upon understanding, goodwill, friendship and mutual cooperation, built up painfully over the years."[20] A similar narrative, though even less justified, is prevailing today on a much larger scale.

Historian Jemar Tisby's central thesis from his 2019 best-seller, *The Color of Compromise*, is illustrative of the way ideology distorts reality by oversim-

---

18. Robin DiAngelo, *What Does It Mean to Be White?: Developing White Racial Literacy* (Lang, Peter, 2016), 64.

19. James Stewart Allen and Philip Sheldon Foner, *American Communism and Black Americans: A Documentary History*, 1919-1929 (Temple University Press, 1987), 9.

20. Manning Johnson, *Color, Communism and Common Sense* (The Alliance, 1958), 54.

plifying it. Tisby states: "History demonstrates that racism never goes away; it just adapts."[21] But, is this conclusion really demonstrated by history, or is it rather a philosophical presupposition about the nature of reality itself? Because racially motivated legal barriers and overt hatred against black people has significantly diminished in the United States since the civil rights era, it would be reasonable to conclude that extremely positive changes have taken place. However, if this were true, it would threaten one of the social justice movement's major reasons for existence. The only way for the movement to continue marching toward racial equity is to pinpoint or produce evidence of inequity.

Thus Tisby points to things like "law-and-order politics," the "wealth gap between black and white citizens," the existence of Confederate monuments, Christian schools with "racially insensitive policies, and the "devaluing of black theology" to prove that racism against black people has adapted in a new era.[22] People who support "state's rights," or speak out against welfare, or say "all lives matter," or support President Trump, or disagree with the assessments and solutions of activists for racial equity are somehow complicit in this racism.[23] Tisby admits that "since the 1970s, Christian complicity in racism has become more difficult to discern." But that is only because "it is hidden" taking on "subtler forms." For Tisby, racism is a "system of oppression" that does not need the "malicious words and actions of individuals" to exist. Rather, it is "prejudice plus power" and "includes the imposition of bigoted ideas."[24]

Philosopher Donald Livingston describes ideologues like Tisby as people who become "obsessed with one ill in society and use that as the key to defining the whole... For critical race theorists it is white supremacy."[25] Because racism is inescapable in this framework, one must craft their entire life around identifying and eradicating it. Some of the sillier examples include identifying things like sheet music, beards, and farmer's markets as examples

21. Jemar Tisby, *The Color of Compromise: The Truth about the American Church's Complicity in Racism* (Zondervan, 2019), 18.

22. Ibid., 158, 198, 200-201, 204-205.

23. Ibid., 168, 190-191.

24. Ibid., 155, 16.

25. Donald Livingston, "What Is Wrong with Ideology," YouTube Video, https://www.youtube.com/watch?v=KkPytBuDriU.

of white supremacy.[26] Jemar Tisby believes the purpose of studying history itself is to change the present through "exposing, explaining, and repairing injustice." Consequently, he encourages young historians to use their craft to assist the "ongoing struggle for liberation from economic, gender, racial or other forms of oppression."[27] This kind of metaphysical tunnel vision distorts both the nature and purpose of historical investigation.

Not only is the scope of research narrowed to focus on one element, such as a particular variety of oppression, but the goal is no longer to understand the past on its own terms. As the great Christian historian Sir Herbert Butterfield stated: "The study of the past with one eye upon the present is the source of all sins and sophistries in history." Though "he can never entirely abstract himself from his own age" a historian "endeavors to understand the past for the sake of the past" and not "for the sake of the present."[28] Tisby and many other activist historians have fallen into the trap of "presentism" whereby they interpret history according to modern priorities, fashions, and values.[29] In this scheme, historical narratives start to resemble simplistic and fanciful cartoons with kernels of truth but lacking depth. Phil Vischer, the creator of the animated children's show Veggie Tales, exhibited this popular flattened reading of history in his "Race in America" video which received over 1.5 million views on YouTube alone.

Vischer starts in the present by identifying the problem he believes history can explain. Black households have only one tenth the wealth of white households. There exists haves and have nots along racial lines. What follows

26. Raven Saunt, "University of Oxford Considers Reforms to 'colonial' Music Curriculum," *Mail Online*, March 28, 2021, https://www.dailymail.co.uk/news/article-9410665/University-Oxford-considers-scrapping-sheet-music-colonial.html; Sean Trainor, "The Racially Fraught History of the American Beard," *The Atlantic*, January 20, 2014, https://www.theatlantic.com/national/archive/2014/01/the-racially-fraught-history-of-the-american-beard/283180/; Douglas Ernst, "Farmers' Markets Called Racist: 'Habits of White People Are Normalized,' Professors Claim," The *Washington Times*, December 27, 2017, sec. Culture, https://www.washingtontimes.com/news/2017/dec/27/farmers-markets-called-racist-habits-of-white-peop/.

27. Jemar Tisby, "History as Activism: Knowing the Past to Change the Present," (History and the Search for Meaning, Calvin University, October 3, 2018), 60:00, 13:00, 53:00.

28. Herbert Butterfield, *The Whig Interpretation of History* (W. W. Norton & Company, 1965), 16, 31.

29. For a full discussion on presentism, see David Hackett Fischer, *Historian's Fallacies* (Harper Collins, 1970), 135-140.

is sixteen minutes of historical illustrations intended to persuade viewers to conclude systemic racism is to blame for the current disparity. Of course, if white racism were the sole cause for this inequality, one would expect that other racial minorities who also experienced discrimination would possess less household income than whites. However, this is not the case.

On average, Americans of Asian descent make more money, have a faster-growing medium income, and possess more wealth than Americans of European descent.[30] Religious American Jews, who are no stranger to historical persecution, possess approximately four and a half times the household net worth of the average American.[31] In addition, black immigrants have a significantly higher income and net-worth than black people born in the United States.[32] To conclude that racism alone caused the wealth gap between white and black people is, at best, a substantial oversimplification that ignores the full picture. Factors such as religion, education, geography, and other cultural considerations may contribute. Unlike Butterfield, who saw history as a "dialectic of different, clashing, or intersecting wills and circumstances," Vischer, like most social justice advocates, only finds one line worth tracing.[33]

Vischer claims white people engineered the wealth gap by creating vagrancy laws, Jim Crow legislation, the Southern Manifesto, segregation academies, law and order rhetoric, the Federal Housing Administration, the G.I. Bill, suburbanization, drug criminalization, discriminatory policing,

---

30. "The Average Net Worth And Income For Asian Americans," Financial Samurai (blog), May 30, 2021, https://www.financialsamurai.com/the-average-net-worth-and-income-for-asian-americans/.

31. Lisa Keister, *Faith and Money: How Religion Contributes to Wealth and Poverty* (Cambridge University Press, 2011), 86.

32. "Increasingly Affluent, Educated and Diverse: African-American Consumers: The Untold Story" (Nielsen, 2015), 13, http://web.archive.org/web/20161114192129/https://www.nielsen.com/content/dam/corporate/us/en/reports-downloads/2015-reports/african-american-consumer-untold-story-sept-2015.pdf; Ken Dubrowski, "The Color of Wealth in Boston," Federal Reserve Bank of Boston, March 25, 2015, https://www.bostonfed.org/publications/one-time-pubs/color-of-wealth.aspx; Monica Anderson, "6 Key Findings about Black Immigration to the U.S.," Pew Research Center, April 9, 2015, https://www.pewresearch.org/fact-tank/2015/04/09/6-key-findings-about-black-immigration/.

33. C. T. McIntire, "Introduction," in *Herbert Butterfield: Writings on Christianity and History* (New York: Oxford University Press, 1979), xxxi.

and education barriers. Yet inaccuracies, exaggerations, limited analysis, and dubious correlations plague his narrative.

For example, Vischer incorrectly states that vagrancy laws were "only applied to black men" and ignores the desperate economic circumstances in which they arose.[34] He neglects to discuss the ways in which some white people promoted integration gradually and the constitutional concerns associated with forced integration.[35] When it comes to disparities in home ownership, Vischer overlooks the historical correlation between income, education and home ownership.[36] He also fails to mention how the FHA Underwriting Manuel's guidelines and racial restrictive covenants applied to more than just black people.[37] In addition, Vischer completely ignores laws prohibiting discrimination on the basis of race in lending as well as studies within the last thirty years that show racial discrimination does not prevent minorities from obtaining loans.[38] Vischer's oversimplifications cause him to make greater errors in evaluating the criminal justice system.

---

34. C. Vann Woodward, *Origins of the New South, 1877-1913: A History of the South* (LSU Press, 1981), 212; Philip Leigh, *Southern Reconstruction* (Westholme Publishing, 2018), 41-44; Robert Somers, *The Southern States Since the War* (Macmillan and Co., 1871), 153.

35. C. Vann Woodward, *The Strange Career of Jim Crow* (Oxford University Press, 2001), 33-37; Michael Bertrand, *Race, Rock, and Elvis* (University of Illinois Press, 2000), Charles Joyner, *Shared Traditions: Southern History and Folk Culture* (University of Illinois Press, 1999); 174-176; 25, 30, 149, 205; William Martin, *A Prophet with Honor: The Billy Graham Story* (Zondervan, 2018), 173-176; Barry Goldwater, *The Conscience of a Conservative* (Victor Publishing Company, 1960), 31-37.

36. Between 1940 and 1980, a narrowing in the "education or income gap [between black and white people] translates directly into a reduction in the [home] ownership gap." See William Collins and Robert Margo, "Race and Home Ownership from the End of the Civil War to the Present," November 2010, 12.

37. "Underwriting Manuel: Underwriting and Valuation Procedure Under Title II of the National Housing Act" (Federal Housing Administration, February 1938); Gwen Aviles, "An Ugly Legacy: Latino Couple Finds Racist Covenant in Housing Paperwork," NBC News, November 14, 2019, https://www.nbcnews.com/news/latino/ugly-legacy-latino-couple-finds-racist-covenant-housing-paperwork-n1082476.

38. The Fair Housing Act of 1968, The Equal Credit Opportunity Act of 1974, the Home Mortgage Discrimination Act of 1975, and the Community Reinvestment Act of 1977 all "created additional protections against redlining." See Amy Hillier, "Redlining and the Homeowners' Loan Corporation," *Journal of Urban History* 29, no. 4 (May 1, 2003): 2; Munnell Alicia et al., "Mortgage Lending in Boston: Interpreting HMDA Data," *American Economic Review* 86, no. 1 (March 1996): 25–53; Harold Black, M. Cary Collins, and

He insinuates that white people's fear of black people created disparities in policing and cites a poll, known to be compromised, which falsely alleges that the majority of Americans blamed black people for crime in 1968.[39] However, he overlooks the fact that many urban black people requested additional law enforcement themselves.[40] Vischer also points to higher incarceration rates as evidence that harsher penalties for drug-related crimes, especially for crack cocaine violations, singled out black people. Yet again, he fails to mention that most of the Congressional Black Caucus supported these harsher measures.[41] Penalties for possessing crystal meth, which is associated with white people, were the same as the penalties for possessing crack cocaine until 2010, at which point they became even more severe.[42]

Vischer insists there is "no visible connection between higher incarceration rates and higher violent crime rates." Yet, only about 17% of black people in prison are there on drug charges. Violent crime is currently the most proportionally significant category in which more black people are incarcerated than white people.[43] The F.B.I. reports that black people account for over 37% of violent crime arrests even though they make up a little over 13% of the population according to the Census Bureau.[44] The Department of Justice found that over 70% of violent crimes against black

---

Ken Cyree, "Do Black-Owned Banks Discriminate against Black Borrowers?," *Journal of Financial Services Research* 11, no. 1 (February 1, 1997): 190.

39. The poll Vischer cited "is probably the most outstanding example of pollster misbehavior on the crime issue in the 1960s." See Keri E. Iyall Smith, *Sociology of Globalization: Cultures, Economies, and Politics* (Avalon Publishing, 2012), 313-314.

40. James Forman, *Locking Up Our Own: Crime and Punishment in Black America* (Farrar, Straus and Giroux, 2017), 10.

41. Jason Riley, "Is The War On Drugs Racist?," *The Federalist*, July 17, 2014, https://thefederalist.com/2014/07/17/is-the-war-on-drugs-racist/.

42. Heather Mac Donald, *The War on Cops: How the New Attack on Law and Order Makes Everyone Less Safe* (Encounter Books, 2017), 155.

43. Total black people incarcerated: 470,100. Violent crime: 256,300. Property: 59,400, Drug: 80,200. Public Order 72,400. Total white people incarcerated: 417,800. Violent crime: 191,800. Property 92,500. Drug: 80,000. Public Order: 72,800. See E. Ann Carson, "Prisoners in 2018," Bureau of Justice Statistics, April 2020, 9, 21-24.

44. "Arrests by Race and Ethnicity, 2018," FBI, accessed July 4, 2021, https://ucr.fbi.gov/crime-in-the-u.s/2018/crime-in-the-u.s.-2018/tables/table-43; "U.S. Census Bureau QuickFacts: United States," April 1, 2020, https://www.census.gov/quickfacts/fact/table/US/POP010220.

people are committed by other black people.[45] Black criminals also commit violent crimes against white victims nine times as often as white criminals do against black victims.[46] It is likely that this data could make more sense of the current 33% incarceration rate among blacks than Vischer's charge of white racism.

Vischer also alleges that a study of drivers in New Jersey showed discrimination on the part of the police since black drivers were stopped 42% of the time though they composed only 15% of drivers. However, the study he references claims that only 32.7% and 22.1% of stops, at different points on the New Jersey Turnpike, were of black people.[47] Vischer also fails to mention another study on the New Jersey turnpike that found "2.7 percent of black drivers were speeders, compared with 1.4 percent of white drivers. Among drivers going faster than 90 m.p.h., the disparity was even greater."[48] Such carelessness in relaying and interpreting data seem to be a common occurrence both for Vischer and social justice advocates arguing for the current existence of systemic racism.

At one point, Vischer falsely attributes the findings in a survey specifically focused on economic conditions experienced by black people who lived in urban areas to black people in general.[49] At another point he cites a study that suggests white teachers are half as likely to recommend a black student for a gifted track. Yet, the very study he mentions admits its own limitations in not considering a school's "gifted referral and evaluation process," which may explain the disparity. It also found that Asian students were overrepresented in gifted programs and "points to a need for additional research"

---

45. Rachel Morgan and Barbara Oudekerk, "Criminal Victimization, 2018," Bureau of Justice Statistics, September 2019, 13.

46. Black on White violent incidents were approximately 547,948.08 while White on Black incidents were approximately 59,777.64. See "Arrests by Race and Ethnicity, 2018," FBI, accessed July 4, 2021, https://ucr.fbi.gov/crime-in-the-u.s/2018/crime-in-the-u.s.-2018/tables/table-43

47. "State v. Soto, 324 N.J. Super. 66" (Casetext, March 4, 1996), https://casetext.com/case/state-v-soto-36.

48. David Kocieniewski, "Study Suggests Racial Gap in Speeding in New Jersey," *The New York Times*, March 21, 2002, sec. B.

49. Roberta Garner and Black Hawk Hancock, *Social Theory: Continuity and Confrontation: A Reader*, Third Edition (University of Toronto Press, 2014), 215-216.

to understand the disparity for black students.[50] Interestingly, in arguing his case, Vischer also leaves out details one assumes a professing Christian would include.

For instance, he mentions nothing about scientific racism including eugenics and Planned Parenthood. In 2018 alone, 117,626 black babies died as the result of abortion procedures. Vischer also skips over the potential harmful effects of socialist-leaning movements and policies.

He fails to mention the racism of the early labor union movement and does not consider the possible negative impact minimum wage has had on black youth unemployment.[51] He ignores President Lyndon B. Johnson's "war on crime" and "Great Society," instead focusing his criticism on Richard Nixon's "war on drugs."

Some conservative economists argue that cultural factors, and the negative impact poverty alleviation policies have on cultural factors, contribute to the wealth gap far more than racism. For almost the first hundred years since the end of slavery, black people advanced themselves economically despite barriers, including racial ones. Between emancipation and the turn-of-the-century, it is estimated that black people increased their income by over 240% and their rate of increase was higher than the general population.[52] By 1900, black families owned or partially owned 25% of the farms they worked.[53] Black-owned businesses doubled from twenty thousand to forty thousand from 1900 to 1914.[54] Before 1960, Black people started over one hundred institutions of higher learning for themselves.[55] According

50. Jason Grissom and Christopher Redding, "Discretion and Disproportionality: Explaining the Underrepresentation of High-Achieving Students of Color in Gifted Programs," AERA Open, January 1, 2016.

51. Walter Williams, *Race & Economics: How Much Can Be Blamed on Discrimination?* (Hoover Press, 2013), 38-48.

52. Robert Higgs, *Competition and Coercion: Blacks in the American Economy 1865-1914* (CUP Archive, 1977), 102.

53. Bruce Reynolds, "Black Farmers in America, 1865-2000: The Pursuit of Independent Farming and the Role of Cooperatives" (United States Department of Agriculture, 2002), 23.

54. August Meier, "Negro Class Structure and Ideology in the Age of Booker T. Washington," Phylon 23, no. 3 (1962): 260.

55. "List of Historically Black Colleges and Universities," https://www.benhillumc.org/wp-content/uploads/2019/12/HBCUs-and-their-Affiliations-12122019.pdf.

to economist Walter Williams: "In every census from 1890 to 1954, blacks were either just as active or more so than whites in the labor market."[56] Some former slaves, such as Alonzo Herndon, Joseph Haygood Blodgett, and Robert Reed Church even became millionaires. While ideologues like Vischer prefer to explain the complexities of history by presupposing oppression as the root cause, it is very likely a more significant element is at work.

A moral breakdown and abandonment of the family unit seem to be major contributors to the current situation. In 1960, not even 8% of black marriages ended in divorce and 67% of black children were born to a married couple.[57] Though black incarceration rates rose over the course of the 20th century, they did not hit over 30% until 1942.[58] Today, over 77% of black children are born to unmarried mothers.[59] One study indicated that "black men were more likely to consume pornography than all other race/gender combinations."[60] Black women on average also have the highest abortion rate of any other demographic.[61] If being raised in a married family reduces a child's probability of living in poverty by around 80%, it follows that policies that weaken the family by encouraging out-of-wedlock births and rewarding unemployment are probably not helping. In fact, though Canada does not have the same history of prejudice against black people as the United States,

56. Walter Williams, "The Black Family Is Struggling, and It's Not Because of Slavery," *The Daily Signal*, September 20, 2017, https://www.dailysignal.com/2017/09/20/black-family-struggling-not-slavery/.

57. M. Belinda Tucker and Claudia Mitchell-Kernan, *The Decline in Marriage Among African Americans: Causes, Consequences, and Policy Implications* (Russell Sage Foundation, 1995), 10; David Ellwood and Jonathan Crane, "Family Change among Black Americans: What Do We Know?," *Journal of Economic Perspectives* 4, no. 4 (December 1990): 67.

58. Patrick Langan, "Race of Prisoners Admitted to State and Federal Institutions, 1926-86" (United States Department of Justice, May 1991).

59. Robert Rector, "Marriage: America's Greatest Weapon Against Child Poverty," The Heritage Foundation, September 16, 2010, https://www.heritage.org/poverty-and-inequality/report/marriage-americas-greatest-weapon-against-child-poverty-0; Paul Bedard, "77% Black Births to Single Moms, 49% for Hispanic Immigrants," *Washington Examiner*, May 5, 2017, https://www.washingtonexaminer.com/77-black-births-to-single-moms-49-for-hispanic-immigrants.

60. Samuel Perry and Cyrus Schleifer, "Race and Trends in Pornography Viewership, 1973-2016: Examining the Moderating Roles of Gender and Religion," *Journal of Sex Research* 56, no. 1 (January 2019): 62–73.

61. Tara Jatlaoui, "Abortion Surveillance – United States, 2015," *Surveillance Summaries* 67, no. 13 (2018).

black people still experience similar disparities in economics, education, incarceration, and family breakdown.[62]

At the end of his presentation, Vischer announces: "I'm not here to tell you what the right solutions are because I don't know."[63] Yet, the information he chose to distort, focus on and leave out guides viewers to conclude that racism is responsible for the wealth gap and white people are to blame. This analysis logically leads to social justice solutions rather than addressing the causes of familial disintegration. When faced with the issue of fatherless homes, Vischer stated it was an issue he could "do very little about." Instead he chose to focus on issues he could affect such as early childhood education and housing access.[64] This is how an egalitarian ideological metaphysic, or understanding of reality, drives a social justice ethic.

Family-driven, free market, or law enforcement remedies are no longer considered because racism is assumed as the only cause behind the gap. Social justice advocates generally do not pursue measures to impede family breakdown by perhaps making abortion illegal, reimplementing anti-pornography measures, and gradually ending the welfare state. Neither do they lobby to enact proposals that afford black teenagers more opportunities by ending minimum wage laws, promoting charter schools, and producing virtuous art. They do not pursue policies that could deter criminal behavior through things like restitution-based punishments or the death penalty. Generally, they argue the opposite side on these issues. This "bias" against conservative solutions is rooted in an alternative conception of reality itself.

Ideology

Today, political conservatives take for granted a "liberal bias" existing in the news, entertainment, and academic industries. Many talk show hosts

---

62. Samuel Sey, "Our Fathers, Our Failures," *Slow To Write*, June 15, 2019, https://slowtowrite.com/our-fathers-our-failures/.

63. Phil Vischer, *Holy Post - Race in America*, 2020, https://www.youtube.com/watch?v=AGUwcs9qJXY&t=19s.

64. Phil Vischer [@philvischer], 2020, "Yes, fatherless is an issue. But it's an issue that I, from the outside, can do very little about. Focusing on issues we can do little about breeds apathy. So I'm focusing on issues I can affect, like early childhood education, housing access, etc.," July 25, 2020, 10:22 a.m., https://twitter.com/philvischer/status/1287030428285702144

spend a great deal of time and energy exposing the media's lies and double standards. Yet, such complaints are only relevant to those who value truth. Christians, of all people, should believe truth matters. After all, the Bible teaches that both "bear[ing] false witness" and using "differing weights and differing measures" are sinful in the eyes of God.[65] Unfortunately, even self-proclaimed Christians often adopt false beliefs due to pragmatic concerns or ideological precommitments.

Historian Carey Roberts describes ideology as a "rationalistic, closed system of thought designed to explain all of human behavior through simple precepts."[66] In other words, ideology explains human nature and activity in total by reducing it to a singular impulse. For Marxists, class conflict motivates human action; for feminists, it is patriarchal domination; and for critical race theorists, it is whiteness. One can see how making one determining principle the exclusive factor in accounting for all human relationships can destroy social bonds by arousing mistrust. Sacrificial actions such as philanthropy, benevolence, and leaving an inheritance for one's children are simply interpreted as ways to advance one's own class, gender, race, or some other quality. In fact, history itself becomes "a series of stages characterized by the singular motivations of the powerful exploiting the powerless."[67]

Philosopher David Hume referred to ideologues as "pretenders of wisdom" who replace "virtuous and tender sentiments" with "a certain sullen pride and contempt of mankind."[68] Often this disposition manifests itself in those who love humanity in the abstract but show little affinity for the particular humans they know personally. They profess "love with word or with tongue" but not "in deed and truth."[69] They may say they care deeply about the condition of the poor and downtrodden but maintain little connection to either. Instead they seek to use institutions of power to achieve a theoretical status for the destitute that often fails to improve actual human lives in any tangible way. Modernity is filled with such examples.

---

65. Ex 20:16; Prov 20:10

66. Clyde Wilson et al., *Exploring the Southern Tradition* (Abbeville Institute Press, 2019), loc 3514, Kindle.

67. Ibid., loc 3518.

68. David Hume, *Essays Moral, Political, and Literary*, vol. 2, 2 vols. (London: Longmans, Green, and Co., 1875), 371.

69. 1 John 3:18

From the way slavery was abolished in the United States, in which an estimated "quarter of the four million freed slaves either died or suffered from illness," to the way strict COVID-19 lockdowns resulted in "more deaths from other causes," some cures are frequently worse than the diseases they are intended to eradicate.[70] Instead of reforming society in natural, gradual, and localized approaches, ideologues reflexively attempt to revolutionize society through immediate and all-encompassing action. Mechanisms of the modern state force their innovations upon humans within their jurisdictions in a posture approaching divinity. This is why many members of "the modern intelligentsia... idoliz[e] those institutions that exercise power" and produce "ideas that best place them in relationship to those powerful institutions."[71]

Because of their reductionist understanding of human nature and appetite for coercion, ideologues tend to incorrectly evaluate situations while suppressing dissidents who question their interpretations. Communist revolutionary Vladimir Lenin believed "the role of a newspaper [was] not limited... to the spreading of ideas" but to organizing "means by which the revolutionary Party could influence... events."[72] Socialist historian Howard Zinn thought the historian's job was to promulgate equality and "change the culture" by siding with victims and imagining "new possibilities." The media could then use this history to promote "a fundamental restructuring of our society."[73] Influential investor and globalist George Soros asked the question, "Why should social science confine itself to passively studying social phenomena when it can be used to actively change the state of affairs?"[74]

---

70. Paul Harris, "How the End of Slavery Led to Starvation and Death for Millions of Black Americans," *The Guardian*, June 16, 2012, http://www.theguardian.com/world/2012/jun/16/slavery-starvation-civil-war; John Tierney, "The Data Shows Lockdowns End More Lives than They Save," *New York Post*, March 22, 2021, https://nypost.com/2021/03/22/the-data-shows-lockdowns-end-more-lives-than-they-save/.

71. Clyde Wilson et al., *Exploring the Southern Tradition* (Abbeville Institute Press, 2019), loc 3514, Kindle.

72. Joseph Stalin, *J. V. Stalin: Works 1921-1923*, vol. 5 (Foreign Languages Publishing House, 1953), 289.

73. Howard Zinn, *The Indispensable Zinn: The Essential Writings of the "People's Historian,"* ed. Timothy McCarthy (The New Press, 2012), 13-14, 73, 75; "Our Interview with the People's Historian, Howard Zinn," *Boulder Weekly*, October 2, 2008, https://www.boulderweekly.com/archives/20081002/howardzinn.html.

74. George Soros, "Transcript: General Theory of Reflexivity" (Central European University, October 26, 2009).

Thus to ideologues, services intended to inform others should not prioritize comprehensive understanding, but rather, political persuasion. Historian Clyde Wilson summarizes the approach in the field of academic history:

> For a long time history was "philosophy teaching by example," that is, the account of men's actions as good or evil in relation to the health of their societies. In the new form of history, actions are not good or evil in themselves, but only to be praised or condemned to the degree they forward or retard progress as defined by ideology. One effect of this is that… historians do not care about the weight of evidence but only about cherry-picking facts to suit the predetermined theory. The duty of historians, they think, is to make a better world, not to tell the truth.[75]

This same tendency can be seen in journalism, entertainment, and many other fields. Even clergymen increasingly resemble community organizers, social workers, and activists more than they do the clerics of yesterday who saw their role as understanding, declaring, and preparing for the world to come. It turns out even Scripture can be easily distorted for political purposes just as the historical record often is. This is why during great advancements for ideological causes, such as the push to sanction homosexual wedding ceremonies or expose men accused of sexually abusing women, popular voices across various outlets and institutions depict issues and situations in a seemingly coordinated fashion. It may be tempting to assume they all receive identical talking points emanating from a smoke-filled room somewhere. However, there is another explanation.

Even without a central authority producing official narratives, those committed to similar ideologies tend to think in the same absolute terms. The result of an event or the legacy of an individual are reduced to black-and-white interpretations. Either a certain condition advances the cause of equality or hinders it. Almost all scenarios are increasingly pushed through this narrow channel of moral evaluation. This shared outlook combined with the social pressure to gain respect from industry leaders reinforces prevailing narratives.

---

75. Wilson, *Exploring the Southern Tradition* , loc 3525.

Exchanging the Truth

Theologian Peter Jones provides helpful categories for understanding the fundamental problem behind ideological thinking. Jones argues that Marxism and its derivatives, such as critical race theory, reject "divinely instituted distinctions" emanating from a "personal Creator God" leaving everything "open to acts of personal power." Instead of viewing physical existence as ordered within a spiritual reality and limited by divine law, design, and providence, Marx declared "human consciousness as the supreme divinity" and set out to create "a utopian egalitarian society based on equity and sameness." This error fits into what the Apostle Paul defined as "exchang[ing] the truth of God for a lie, and worship[ing] and serv[ing] the creature rather than the Creator."[76]

Jones describes this usurpation in which men treat themselves as god and enforce the principles of their own imaginations onto the world as a version of "Oneism." In Oneism, everything "shares the same essential nature" such as power or material. There is no distinction between Creator and creation. It is up to fallible human minds to create meaning, define the essence of justice, grant rights, and validate truth. Humans attain significance through struggling through mechanisms, such as the Hegelian dialectic, to achieve a truly just society in this world.

Conversely, in "Twoism... creation shares a certain essence" but "God is a completely different being whose will determines the nature and function of all created things."[77] Christian apologist Nancy Pearcey explains that because there is a transcendent Creator, there is no "need to ramrod everything into a limited set of categories derived from one part of the cosmic order. Christianity... affirms the high dignity of humans as full persons made in the image of a personal God."[78] Thus, instead of viewing humans as simply the product of social forces who occupy various degrees of oppression, Twoism acknowledges the complex and important range of identities, beliefs, behaviors, relationships, responsibilities, talents, positions, and personalities people designed by God possess.

---

76. Rom 1:25

77. Peter Jones, *One Or Two: Seeing a World of Difference, Romans 1 for the Twenty-First Century* (Main Entry Editions, 2010), loc 132-142, Kindle.

78. Finding Truth, 51.

Oppression is an inescapable part of the fallen human condition. Until the redeemed live in a new heaven and a new earth, humans will always sin against other humans and justify their sin based on many factors including social and physical characteristics. But not everything boils down to power dynamics. All that exists cannot be quantified into a computer-like world of colors representing different forms of oppression and numbers representing oppression levels. Many different forces converge to shape circumstances according to the hand of Providence.

As Clyde Wilson states concerning the discipline of history: "History is not an expression of abstract laws, or the record of progress. It is a description of the actions of men, of life, which in turn is an expression of the (partly unknowable) mind of God."[79] Yet, whether it be history, journalism, or social science, the study of mankind should not be a barometer fueled by activists to measure how far humanity has to march in order to achieve egalitarianism. If the goal is truly understanding, it should be a record of the Creator's unfolding plan documented by passive observers. This does not mean that influential opinion shapers are completely unbiased in their observations.

For example, the biblical authors also used narrative to describe the world. Yet, in so doing they accepted the reality of the Divine plan as the term "fullness of time" suggests.[80] Their understanding of God and His law that governs creation influenced their interpretations. They also drew inspiration from symbols of social unity.[81] If anything is needed today, it is historians and journalists who take seriously their responsibility to represent the whole truth while recognizing elements that foster public virtue and social unity. In this way, they can make a positive impact without sacrificing truth or falling into ideological myopia.

---

79. Clyde Wilson, *Defending Dixie: Essays in Southern History and Culture* (Foundation for American Education, 2006), 34.

80. Gal 4:4; Eph 1:10

81. Psalm 78:4; Josh 4:6; Deut 32:7; Rom 15:4; 1 Cor 10:11

CHAPTER 6

SOCIAL JUSTICE ETHICS

WHEREAS SOCIAL JUSTICE advocates tend to assign a value to every conceivable object based on whether or not it advances their egalitarian goals, Christianity teaches that creation is intrinsically valuable because it reflects and glorifies its Creator. The book of Genesis records how God declared everything "He had made" to be "very good" on the sixth day of creation. The book of Colossians explains that not only did God create all things, but "all things were created... for Him." Creation tells of God's glory, design, power, and nature.[1] Augustine of Hippo stated that it was "not with respect to our conveniences or discomfort, but with respect to their own nature, that the creatures are glorying to their Artificer."[2] In other words, the created order, with all its objects and arrangements, is valuable in and of itself regardless of how it furthers the goals of mankind for equality or otherwise.

Society and the Created Order

In a special way, God also made humans in His image. This is why they possess identity, rationality, a conscience, and ultimately a soul. It is why God uniquely governs the affairs of mankind through His moral law and forbids the unjustified taking of human life.[3] Christians have long maintained

---

1. Gen 1:31; John 1:3; Col 1:16; Rom 11:36; Psalm 19:1; Rom 1:20

2. Saint Augustine, *The City of God: A Treaty of Christian Philosophy by St. Augustine of Hippo* (BoD - Books on Demand, 2018), 308.

3. Gen 1:27, 9:6; James 3:9; 2 Peter 2:12

that even evil souls possess intrinsic worth by nature of God creating them. Augustine said that God did not "withhold the bestowal of His goodness" even from the "creature He foreknew [would]… persist in the will to sin."[4] Being made in God's image is one way in which all people share a measure of equality.

Another way in which all people are equal concerns their spiritual condition. Scripture teaches that all humans possess a sin nature and are therefore equally in need of God's forgiveness. The Apostle Paul asserted, "For as in Adam all die, so also in Christ all will be made alive."[5] Since the beginning of Christianity, the teaching that all people are guilty of violating God's law and in need of redemption through Christ inspired numerous missionary movements, just as the notion of all people being made in God's image produced hospitals and charities. This Christian love for people, who often existed outside the natural affections of familiarity, was not primarily motivated by a sense of equality. Rather, it was spurred through a relationship to the Creator that resulted in an appreciation for His creation.[6]

Scripture teaches that a true love for others is specifically represented in God's moral law. Jesus commanded His followers, "In everything, therefore, treat people the same way you want them to treat you, for this is the Law and the Prophets." James, Jesus' half-brother, affirmed that loving one's neighbor fulfilled "the royal law according to the Scripture." Likewise, the Apostle Paul described "love" as the "fulfillment of the law."[7] God's law reflects His own moral character. It also assumes the existence of certain social hierarchies in which this love is applied.

For instance, the Bible commands progeny to honor their father and mother. This command extends to things like maintaining property lines, supporting one's parents in material ways, and the civil magistrate implementing legal prohibitions against cursing them.[8] None of these divine directives would make any sense outside the relationship that exists between parents and offspring.

---

4. Saint Augustine, *Augustine: On the Free Choice of the Will, On Grace and Free Choice, and Other Writings* (Cambridge University Press, 2010), 84.

5. 1 Cor 15:22

6. Matt 5:44; 1 John 4:7-12

7. Matt 7:12; James 2:8; Rom 13:10

8. Ex 20:12; Prov 22:28; Matt 15:3-6; Ex 21:17

Scripture portrays some hierarchies, such as mankind's dominion over nature, a husband's headship over his wife, and parent's authority over their children, as fundamentally rooted in the Creator's perfect design.[9] Other hierarchal relationships, like rulers and subjects, borrowers and lenders, and masters and slaves, are regulated by God's commands but not depicted as fundamentally rooted in creation.[10] Scripture likewise upholds distinctions like national borders, walls, property lines, inheritance, private property, and gender and sexual norms. It also records numerous examples of both people and groups receiving certain advantages based on factors such as age, citizenship, nationality, birth order, appearance, position, level of wisdom, etc.[11] Such realities and the biblical laws that regulate much of them are incompatible with the "equity, diversity, and inclusion" promoted by social justice activists. Many of the pioneers for egalitarian causes understood this.

For example, Karl Marx said, "The social principles of Christianity preach the necessity of a ruling and an oppressed class… [They] are cringing, but the proletariat is revolutionary."[12] Early feminist Elizabeth Cady Stanton stated, "The strongest adverse influence to [woman's] elevation comes from the church, judging from its Biblical expositions."[13] William Lloyd Garrison, a prominent immediate abolitionist, believed: "All reforms are anti-Bible."[14] Antonio Gramsci wanted "socialism" to "kill Christianity" and replace any charitable relationship between the privilege and unprivileged with "class solidarity" and "world domination."[15] Michel Foucault desired to liberate

---

9. Gen 1:28, 2:15, 18, 24; Ex 20:12, Eph 5:22-33, 6:1-4; Zachary Garris, *Masculine Christianity* (Reformation Zion Publishing, 2021), loc 2499-2512, Kindle.

10. Rom 13:1-7; Prov 22:7; Titus 2:9-10

11. Num 34:2-12; Deut 32:8, Acts 17:26; Prov 25:28; Neh 2:17; Deut 19:14; Prov 13:22; Matt 20:15; Acts 5:4; 1 Cor 11:4-15; Rom 1:27; Lev 19:32; 1 Timothy 5:1; Ex 21:2; Acts 22:25-26; Deut 15:6; Rom 9:13; Deut 21:15-17, Lev 21:17; 1 Sam 9:2; 1 Tim 5:17; 1 Thess 5:12; Acts 23:5; Ex 22:28; Prov 24:5-6; Luke 6:40

12. Karl Marx and Friedrich Engels, *Basic Writings on Politics and Philosophy*, ed. Lewis Feuer (Doubleday, 1959), 268-269.

13. Elizabeth Cady Stanton, "Has Christianity Benefited Woman?," *North American Review*, 1885, http://womenwriters.digitalscholarship.emory.edu/content.php?level=div&id=stanton_christianity_001&document=stanton_christianity.

14. Donna Behnke, *Religious Issues in Nineteenth Century Feminism* (Whitston Publishing Company, 1982), 97.

15. Antonio Gramsci, *Sotto La Mole 1916-1920* (CreateSpace Independent Publishing Platform, 2021), 161-162.

people from "political rationality," which he believed stood "on the idea of [Christian] pastoral power."[16]

Love Thy Neighbor

Such sentiments demonstrate an irreconcilable chasm existing between biblical and egalitarian-inspired ethics. Standing behind these broad conceptions lie conflicting understandings of love and justice. Social justice activists tend to think of love as defending and affirming an individual's freedom to define and express themselves. The assumption is that individual's deserve to reach what they believe to be their full potential unhindered by external barriers. Under this thinking, society must adopt and implement a forced equality to eliminate disparities and prevent bigotries associated with certain institutions and associations from preventing individual self-realization.

This framework is often presented as opposing hierarchy and individualism in favor of personal freedom and the common good. However, because it inevitably posits a centralized authority to enforce an abstract equality originating from individual human minds, it is actually both very hierarchical and individualistic. Theoretically, instead of families, churches, businesses, etc. all sharing control, the only major power-disparity that exists is between the individual and the totalitarian State. This construction directly interferes with both a Christian conception of love and justice.

Christians think of love as a quality emanating from God and perfectly exemplified in Jesus' sacrifice and submission to the Father's will. The Apostle Paul described it as a trait that seeks the well-being of others instead of its own interest.[17] Attached to the idea of love is a recognition of divine purpose, duty, and sacrifice. Nevertheless, even though it is the greatest enduring virtue, human love is not intended to eradicate every problem existing in the temporal world.

For example, this side of heaven, poverty will never cease to exist. Subverting God's law by eliminating protections for private property will not achieve this end either. Jesus said "you [will] always have the poor with you"

---

16. Michel Foucault, "Omnes et Singulatim: Towards a Criticism of 'Political Reason'" (The Tanner Lectures on Human Values, Stanford University, October 1979), 254, https://tannerlectures.utah.edu/_documents/a-to-z/f/foucault81.pdf.

17. 1 John 4:16; John 15:13; 1 Cor 13

and instructed His followers not to steal. In the Parable of the Laborers, Jesus' upheld the right of a landowner to do what he wished with what he owned. Rather than entertaining man-centered utopian schemes, Christians attempt to follow Jesus' example in personally giving to the poor.[18] This requires much more of a sacrifice, and often personal investment, than simply voting for a central authority to involuntarily redistribute the resources of others. Given these different conceptions of love, it should come as no surprise that religious and conservative people donate to charity on average much more than non-religious and liberal people in the United States, though they tend to have less money.[19]

This Christian duty to love is also arranged by God according to responsibility and proximity. Jesus taught, "Greater love has no one than this, that one lay down his life for his friends." Paul said, "Let us do good to all people, and especially to those who are of the household of the faith." He also instructed husbands to "love their own wives as their own bodies" and provide especially for those living in their own household.[20] Moses, Jeremiah, Esther, Jesus, and Paul all exhibited a special love for their own nation.[21] Saint Ambrose of Milan, an early Christian leader, believed love should be directed first to God, "then our parents, then our children, and lastly those our household."[22] This way of ranking love's obligations reflects Jesus' command to love neighbor.

---

18. Matt 20:15; 19:21; 29:11; Mark 10:19; John 12:5-6

19. Bradford Richardson, "Religious People More Likely to Give to Charity, Study Shows," The Washington Times, October 30, 2017, sec. Faith & Family, https://www.washingtontimes.com/news/2017/oct/30/religious-people-more-likely-give-charity-study/; Nicholas Kristof, "Opinion | Bleeding Heart Tightwads," The New York Times, December 21, 2008, sec. Opinion, https://www.nytimes.com/2008/12/21/opinion/21kristof.html; David Masci, "How Income Varies among U.S. Religious Groups," Pew Research Center, October 11, 2016, https://www.pewresearch.org/fact-tank/2016/10/11/how-income-varies-among-u-s-religious-groups/; Andy Green, "The Growing Divide: Red States vs. Blue States," Georgetown Public Policy Review, February 21, 2020, http://gppreview.com/2020/02/21/growing-divide-red-states-vs-blue-states/.

20. John 15:13; Gal 6:10; Eph 5:28; 1 Tim 5:8

21. Saint John Chrysostom, *Commentary on the Epistle to the Galatians, and Homilies on the Epistle to the Ephesians, of S. John Chrysostom* (Parker, 1879), 177; Jer 8:21-22; Esther 7:4; 8:6; Matt 15:24; 23:37; Rom 9:2-4

22. St. Thomas Aquinas, *Summa Theologica: Second Part of the Second Part*, ed. Anthony Uyl (Ontario, CA: Devoted Publishing, 2018), 127.

The Greek term translated in English as neighbor means "one who is near."[23] It is true that Jesus commanded Christians to ensure their love for Him exceeded their love for family members.[24] Yet, this was an affirmation of familial love, not a rejection of it. The love springing forth from natural relationships is the foundation for understanding how to love even one's enemies.[25] Early Church Father John Chrysostom asked, "For if a man deserts those who are united by ties of kindred and affinity, how shall he be affectionate towards others?"[26] Ambrose said, "Good-will starts first with those at home, that is with children, parents, brothers, and goes on from one step to another throughout the world."[27]

This preference for one's own family, neighbor, and nation contradicts the premium modern social justice places on preferring those who are different. Influential institutions increasingly celebrate "diversity" while condemning patriarchy and nationalism. If advocates for social justice desire Christianity at all, it is a man-centered version that weakens natural relationships and flattens personal affections into caring for all humans across the globe equally. In a sense, social justice reasoning can replace a love for one's relatives and neighbors with a love for abstractions and fantasies. The current hostility toward "nationalism" illustrates this.

Christian Nationalism

Although today's activists for social justice condemn nationalism, an understanding of the history surrounding the term helps in explaining just what kind of nationalism they object to. It should be noted at the outset that there is a kind of nationalism that seeks social justice by manipulating the familiar love one has for their own people into a love for the State or a set of

23. Douglas Mangum et al., eds., *Lexham Theological Wordbook*, Lexham Bible Reference Series (Bellingham, WA: Lexham Press, 2014), Logos Digital Edition.

24. Matt 10:37

25. Matt 5:43-48

26. Saint John Chrysostom, *The Homilies of S. John Chrysostom: Archbishop of Constantinople, on the Epistles of St. Paul the Apostle to Timothy, Titus, and Philemon* (Parker, 1843), 115.

27. Philip Schaff, *Nicene and Post-Nicene Fathers: Second Series, Volume X Ambrose* (Cosimo, Inc., 2007), 29.

universal propositions. The term "nationalism" became mainstream during the Progressive Era as a "kind of socialism" that supported "equality in distribution" while side-stepping class conflict by appealing to all classes.[28] Edward Bellamy popularized its usage in his extremely popular utopian novel *Looking Backward*, which sparked the creation of *The Nationalist* magazine and over 500 "Bellamy Clubs" across the country.[29]

Bellamy defined nationalism as believing economic and social solutions were found in the "idea" that a united people could use their "collective strength for the common welfare" through nationalizing industry, providing a living wage, and becoming a "universal insurance company" against "injustice, oppression, sickness, age, accident, and disability of every sort."[30] Edward Bellamy's younger cousin, Francis Bellamy, promoted these ideas and eventually wrote the Pledge of Allegiance.[31] In some ways, this kind of nationalism foreshadowed the National Socialists German Workers' Party of the 1930s and glimpses of it can still be seen today especially on the political left.

Not only do members of the Democrat Party generally believe in Bellamy's economic program, but they also share his love for collective power over negative individual rights and local control. This is the kind of nationalism that elevates the centralized authority to a level approaching deity by automatically looking to it to solve the country's problems and granting it the right to define the common good for everyone.

In the wake of the protest for election integrity on January 6, 2021, Speaker of the House Nancy Pelosi expressed her horror at seeing the "desecration" of the National Capitol, which she called "our temple of democracy."[32]

---

28. Richard Theodore Ely, *Socialism: An Examination of Its Nature, Its Strength and Its Weakness, with Suggestions for Social Reform* (T. Y. Crowell & Company, 1894), 87-88.

29. "News of the Movement," *The Nationalist* (1891), 114.

30. William Dwight Porter Bliss, *The Encyclopedia of Social Reform* (Funk & Wagnells Company, 1897), 918.

31. Jeffrey Jones and Peter Meyer, *The Pledge: A History of the Pledge of Allegiance* (St. Martin's Publishing Group, 2010), 53.

32. Nancy Pelosi [@SpeakerPelosi], 2021, "On Jan 6, one of the darkest days in our history, our temple of democracy was attacked by insurrectionists. The gleeful desecration of our Capitol resulted in multiple deaths, physical harm to over 140 members of law enforcement and trauma among staff, support workers & Members.," May 14, 2021, 1:04 p.m., https://twitter.com/SpeakerPelosi/status/1393250809098481667.

President Joe Biden referred to the Capitol as "sacred ground."[33] The media echoed this prioritization of the National Capitol over the thousands of local businesses and hundreds of monuments devastated during the Black Lives Matter protests less than a year before, including the taking over of government buildings in Seattle to form an "Autonomous Zone."[34] There is one form of nationalism still alive and well, and it does not favor the regular, ordinary people residing in a nation. Rather, it owes its allegiance to the collective will as allegedly expressed by a distant all-powerful State. Nevertheless, there is a kind of nationalism social justice advocates despise.

Since the second world war, progressives gradually became suspicious of civic rituals celebrating American identity or drawing inspiration from much of its past. In a recent televised interview, ESPN writer-at-large Bill Rhoden criticized enjoying the Olympics opening ceremony because "nationalism is not good" and displaying the American Flag was associated with the "capitol riots" and the desire to exclude others. Instead of focusing on winning, Rhoden stated the Olympics should be about "soul searching" and "protest." Even thinking the United States should win in basketball was evidence of "entitlement and privilege."[35] Such thinking seems entirely opposed to the main purpose of the Olympics: competition between nations. Yet a veteran sports journalist could not even root for his own country because of how it conflicted with his love for diversity, equity, and inclusion.

This disdain for American symbols is grounded in a globalist mindset that views the existence of people who prefer their own nation over others as exclusive and hateful. In the lead-up to the 2020 election, political strategist James Carville expressed his hope that in beating President Trump, Democrats would "defeat the idea that the United States of America is a place

33. Joe Biden, "Inaugural Address by President Joseph R. Biden, Jr.," https://www.whitehouse.gov/briefing-room/speeches-remarks/2021/01/20/inaugural-address-by-president-joseph-r-biden-jr/.

34. Over 360 businesses in Minneapolis and St. Paul alone were "vandalized, looted or had doors and windows smashed" in the wake of violent protest following George Floyd's death. See Brian Flood, "Minnesota Newspaper Lists over 360 Local Businesses Destroyed by Riots," *Fox News*, June 3, 2020, https://www.foxnews.com/media/minnesota-newspaper-lists-over-360-local-businesses-destroyed-by-riots-with-maps-specific-details-of-damage.

35. Bill Rhoden, *Legendary sportswriter Bill Rhoden discusses Team USA's rocky start at the Olympics and why he thinks the games should've been cancelled.*, July 26, 2021, https://www.facebook.com/watch/?v=4308531315849926.

and not an idea." To Carville, the source of conflict between races, genders, and sexual orientations stemmed from a love for a familiar place with its traditions and hierarchies. Eliminating national animosity meant ditching a love for one's homeland in favor of universal egalitarian principles.[36] Social justice enthusiasts generally assume loving people who share familiar traits means hating those who do not share such traits. However, major Christian thinkers usually thought learning to love those chosen by Providence as neighbors is the first step in loving people who are different or distant.

In contrast, many of the people considered to be modern evangelical leaders today joined the anti-nationalist bandwagon. Just a few examples include Beth Moore, who called "Christian nationalism" the most dangerous idolatrous threat facing the "saints of God" she had ever seen; Lecrae, who declared he was on the "right side of history" for being "anti-Christian nationalism;" and Tim Keller, who said "Christian nationalists" were wrong to preserve their influence by raising money and vilifying "gay activists."[37] Other popular figures such as Jemar Tisby, Ekemini Uwan, and Daniel Hill smeared Christian nationalism as a form of white supremacy.[38] The common

36. John Melendez [@stutteringjohnm], 2020, "@realDonaldTrump I was just talking to @JamesCarville and he said you are going to get your fat ass beat. #Biden2020 @ CaslerNoel," May 21, 2020, 6:15 p.m., https://twitter.com/stutteringjohnm/status/1263594299985281030.

37. Beth Moore [@BethMooreLPM], 2020, "I do not believe these are days for mincing words. I'm 63 1/2 years old & I have never seen anything in these United States of America I found more astonishingly seductive & dangerous to the saints of God than Trumpism. This Christian nationalism is not of God. Move back from it.," Dec 13, 2020, 9:50 a.m., https://twitter.com/BethMooreLPM/status/1338134290647953410; Lecrae [@lecrae], 2021, "Which of course is the anti-racism, pro life from womb to the tomb, care for the marginalized, anti-Christian nationalism, anti- abuse of power side.," Jan 20, 2021, 10:13 a.m., https://twitter.com/lecrae/status/1351910852841103365; Tim Keller, *Timothy Keller: How to Know if You Are a Christian Nationalist*, interview by Jason Daye, March 3, 2021, 00:16, https://www.youtube.com/watch?v=o4M_K5vmDc8.

38. Jemar Tisby [@stutteringjohnm], 2020, "The Christians hollering about Critical Race Theory have invented an enemy that they can decry and use to stoke fear. Meanwhile the real enemy within the camp is white supremacist Christian Nationalism but it's so familiar to them they don't even recognize the threat.," March 6, 2021, 8:30 a.m., https://twitter.com/JemarTisby/status/1368192331829088268; Ekemini Uwan [@sista_theology], 2021, "It's always 'white christian nationalism' and not 'white supremacist christianity.'," Jan 11, 2021, 6:02 p.m., https://twitter.com/BethMooreLPM/status/1338134290647953410; Daniel Hill [@danielhill1336], 2021, "Rejecting White Christian nationalism is not the same thing as rejecting Christianity," Jan 10, 2021, 10:06 p.m., https://twitter.com/stutteringjohnm/status/1263594299985281030.

thread setting "Christian nationalism" apart from "nationalism" seems to be a general notion that one of the chief defining traits of America is its Christianity. Interestingly, by this standard many of the Founders, including the "Father of our Country," were Christian nationalists.

In 1796, George Washington stated in his Farewell Address that Americans, though they possessed "slight shades of difference," shared "the same religion, manners, habits, and political principles."[39] The religion Washington referred to of course was Christianity. This does not mean that everyone in America was an orthodox believer or that someone could not become a citizen unless they signed a statement of faith, though nine of the 13 states did originally require a religious test in order to hold political office.[40] What it meant was that, in general, Americans were culturally Christian and this was one reality that bound them together. As the English philosopher Sir Roger Scruton rightly observed, "Religion is a way of life, involving customs and ceremonies that validate what matters to us, and which reinforce the attachments by which we live."[41] Without a general investment in a mutually shared homeland, history, posterity, religion, and legal system, there is no basis for the trust necessary to form and preserve a society.

According to Scripture, the formation of nations was God's idea. After Noah's flood, the book of Genesis teaches that God formed distinct and separate nations according to land, language, and family. He also made a special covenant with the nation of Israel, to whom He gave land, traditions, an inheritance, religious rituals, and civil laws. The Apostle Paul declared that God made "every nation," including setting their time of existence and national boundaries. The Great Commission itself assumes Christians are to "make disciples of all the nations." In the book of Revelation, the Apostle John revealed that at the consummation of time it would not be an undefined group of people devoid of cultural attachments praising God "before the throne," but rather "a great multitude... from every nation and all tribes

39. George Washington, "Transcript of President George Washington's Farewell Address," 1796, https://www.ourdocuments.gov/doc.php?flash=false&doc=15&page=transcript.

40. "Religious Tests and Oaths in State Constitutions, 1776-1784" (University of Wisconsin-Madison), accessed July 31, 2021, https://csac.history.wisc.edu/document-collections/religion-and-the-ratification/religious-test-clause/religious-tests-and-oaths-in-state-constitutions-1776-1784/.

41. Roger Scruton, *Our Church: A Personal History of the Church of England* (Atlantic Books, 2014), 15.

and peoples and tongues."[42] As can be seen, God's sovereign purpose is for families to organically form nations over time as children are born and habits form.

Loving one's own people is part of loving the Creator and His creation. It also reflects a recognition of God's particular plan in an individual's life and the obligations that come with it. The Protestant Reformer John Calvin, in commenting on the Parable of the Good Samaritan, acknowledged the truth that "we ought to embrace the whole human race without exception in a single feeling of love." Yet he also stated:

> I do not deny that the more closely a man is linked to us, the more intimate obligation we have to assist him. It is the common habit of mankind that the more closely men are bound together by the ties of kinship, of acquaintanceship, or of neighborhood, the more responsibilities for one another they share. This does not offend God; for his providence, as it were, leads us to it.[43]

Today's social justice movement seeks to replace this familiar love, not with a love for tangible people in distant places, but rather, with a love for achieving an ever increasing yet always elusive, diverse society. In essence, social justice thinking compels one to love an idea in their own mind camouflaged as love for others. Christianity, on the other hand, actually directs love toward real people. Additionally, love is not the only quality that arranges itself according to purpose and responsibility. Justice also operates within a hierarchal framework.

Equality and Justice for All

Two general concepts emerge from the multiple Greek and Hebrew words translated in English Bibles as "justice." The first relates to personal conduct. Someone who impartially fulfills their moral duty before God toward others is a just (or righteous) person. The second concept relates more to the

---

42. Gen 10:2-5; 20; 31-32; 11:7-9; 12:1-3; Psalm 135:12; Ex 12:14; Josh 4:6; Num 36:9; Deut 32:9; Acts 17:26; Matt 28:19; Rev 7:9-10

43. John Calvin, *Institutes of the Christian Religion*, ed. John T. McNeill (Westminster John Knox Press, 1960), 418.

impartial decisions made by rulers, especially in a civil capacity.[44] Scripture teaches that God exemplifies both ideas. Deuteronomy 32:4 declares: "The Rock! His work is perfect, For all His ways are just; A God of faithfulness and without injustice, Righteous and upright is He." God is an impartial judge who acts in accordance with His own righteous standard.[45]

While love compels one to sacrifice themselves for the good of others, justice causes them to give others their due, whether reward or punishment, regardless of affiliation or personal feeling. The biblical authors often acknowledged groups like strangers, widows, orphans, and the poor as especially susceptible to injustice because they lacked the natural protections that accompany being part of a familiar culture and family structure or did not possess the resources necessary to pursue justice if wronged. Yet the righteous response to this disparity was not to rig social systems in their favor, but rather to fear God and voluntarily engage in personal charity.[46]

In Exodus 23, God even condemns perverting justice by showing partiality based on factors such as personal gain, peer pressure, compassion for the poor, hatred for enemies, preference for one's family, and opportunities to take advantage of strangers. Leviticus 19 likewise states: "You shall do no injustice in judgment; you shall not be partial to the poor nor defer to the great, but you are to judge your neighbor fairly."[47] The principle of faithfully applying a just standard toward someone irrespective of their identity is often called "equality before the law." This concept produced things like due process, trial by jury, and judicial recusal in our legal systems, which have a unique responsibility to publicly apply justice.

The Protestant Reformer Martin Luther identified "three hierarchies ordained by God," which were the "the house," the "worldly government," and "the Church." Each had unique responsibilities according to their intended purpose and jurisdiction. Luther believed the "secular government"

---

44. Robert Laird Harris, Gleason Archer, and Bruce Waltke, *Theological Wordbook of the Old Testament* (Moody Press, 1980), 188, 948, 1879; Gerhard Kittel, Gerhard Friedrich, and Geoffrey Bromiley, *Theological Dictionary of the New Testament: Abridged in One Volume* (Wm. B. Eerdmans Publishing, 1985), 169, 171, 469-473.

45. Gen 18:25; Ecc 3:17; Psalm 25:9; 2 Tim 4:8; common Hebrew nouns translated as "justice": *tsedeq, mishpat*; common Greek nouns translated as "justice": *dikaiosune, krisis*.

46. Lev 23:22; Deut 27:19; Psalm 82:3-4; Isa 1:17; Zech 7:9-10; Acts 20:35

47. Ex 23:1-9; Lev 19:15

was to "judge, protect, and promote land and people."[48] The Apostle Paul taught that government was "established by God" as a "minister" to bring "wrath on the one who practices evil."[49] Many Christian thinkers refer to government's unique calling as a "ministry of justice."[50] This means that the civil magistrate, unlike the family and the church, possesses a unique role in applying justice in society. Not all the commands and responsibilities given to individuals, families, or churches apply to the government. Neither are all the actions associated with the government's role appropriate for other jurisdictions. Social justice advocates tend to minimize these distinctions by prioritizing their egalitarian objectives over civil order.

One of the most common examples of this involves churches that consider it their primary purpose to implement justice for the temporal realm rather than maintain a ministry of grace for the eternal realm. For decades mainline denominations progressively substituted the gospel and discipleship for a social gospel and activism. More recently this trend is impacting the evangelical world. Social justice initiatives are elevated and mixed with spiritual categories.

Danny Akin recently summarized the current sentiment when he stated that Southeastern Seminary focuses on "bringing the presence of the kingdom now" by "building churches on earth that look like the [ethnically diverse] church in heaven."[51] From the pages of *Christianity Today*, the former editor-in-chief Mark Galli argued that the "goal of social justice" was the same as "evangelism."[52] Ed Stetzer, the executive director of the Billy Graham Center at Wheaton College, believes that "Scripture teaches us to be people who are so shaped by the gospel that we live as good news by

---

48. Martin Luther, *Martin Luther's Basic Theological Writings* (Fortress Press, 2012), 574.

49. Rom 13:3-4

50. Greg Bahnsen, *By This Standard: The Authority of God's Law Today* (American Vision, 2015), 191; Donald McKim, *John Calvin: A Companion to His Life and Theology* (Wipf and Stock Publishers, 2015), 148.

51. Danny Akin, Walter Strickland, and Mark Liederbach, *A Conversation Regarding Theology, Ethics, and Racial Injustice*, interview by Ken Keathley, June 5, 2020, 20:40, https://www.youtube.com/watch?v=cFsOZhu_E_s.

52. Mark Galli, "Evangelism Is a Work of Social Justice," *Christianity Today*, September 13, 2018, https://www.christianitytoday.com/ct/2018/september-web-only/keeping-social-justice-ministries-vibrant.html.

engaging in social justice."[53] The popular "Just Gospel" conferences, which host some of the biggest names in evangelicalism, such as David Platt, Russell Moore, and J.D. Greear, characteristically focus on social justice. Modern Christianity's shift away from the eternal and toward the temporal is not just the result of confusing the church's and the government's roles in society. Ultimately, the disagreement between today's revolution and traditional Christianity involves competing versions of justice.

Activists on the left see justice as a means to eliminate disparities and ultimately reach a state of social equality. In order to accomplish this goal, partiality is unavoidable. Lady Justice must remove her blindfold and consider external factors such as race, class, gender, orientation, and age in order to render a just verdict. The changes necessary to reach equality inevitably require the redistribution of influence, privilege, or resources. Sometimes this is achieved through illegal or immediate action by any means necessary. This arrangement essentially replaces justice with envy and covetousness. It is also diametrically opposed to biblical understandings of personal responsibility, private property, and hierarchal arrangements.

The main reason today's activists think justice should produce egalitarian equality instead of equality before the law is that they believe, like Rousseau, that mankind is essentially good and society, with all its structures and institutions, is corrupted. Liberating humanity from enslavement to various social hierarchies is the only way to create a world that values diversity, equity, and inclusion. This is likely one reason many Christian leaders think of themselves as "engaging culture" from the outside. If they separate themselves from the rest of society and prove the church is also in favor of social justice, the revolution may consider them allies and not enemies.

For example, Jonathan Leeman of 9Marks ministries called "identity politics... an unexpected ally."[54] J.D. Greear described himself as a complementarian who also somehow believed in the "tearing down of all hierarchy."[55] Influential author Tim Keller routinely portrays authentic

---

53. "Ed Stetzer," interview by Zach Nielsen, October 3, 2009, https://www.youtube.com/watch?v=EV1psK8MoFM&t=19s.

54. Jonathan Leeman, "Identity Politics and the Death of Christian Unity," *9Marks*, April 15, 2020, https://www.9marks.org/article/identity-politics-and-the-death-of-christian-unity/.

55. J.D. Greear [@jdgreear], 2018, "Thank you, Beth! Hoping that we are entering a new era where we in the complementarian world take all the Word of God seriously—not

Christianity as a religion that rejects any form of social power.[56] Pastors like David Platt and John Piper teach it is morally acceptable to vote for candidates in favor of social justice despite their positions in conflict with Christian ethics such as favoring abortion.[57] All of these examples accommodate the social justice movement and fulfill the desires of many secular egalitarian leaders who, instead of rejecting Christianity because of its hierarchal teaching, pursued avenues whereby they could redefine religion to suite their objectives.

Jean-Jacques Rousseau believed "Christian law" was "harmful" to the "constitution of a state." Instead, he imagined a religion that would "one day make a revolution among men." Rather than biblical revelation, Rousseau based his new faith on the "innate principle of justice and virtue." Rousseau stated, "I think that each will be judged, not on what he believed but on what he did." Political thinker Arthur Melzer rightly pointed out that this belief "entails a great secularization" by making "morality—man's free moral action in this world—the highest thing."[58]

Herbert Marcuse also had problems with traditional religion. He believed it inspired guilt in the present life, postponed human fulfillment to the afterlife, and reinforced the evil status-quo, including things like the holocaust and Vietnam War. Yet he also held out hope that religion could be beneficial in transforming society if it became a heretical "expression of a political attitude" that protested prevailing standards with a practical message for "here on earth!"[59]

Likewise, Derrick Bell believed "fundamentalist Christians divert polit-

---

just the parts about distinction of roles but also re: the tearing down of all hierarchy & his gracious distribution of gifts to all his children!," May 5, 2018, 3:03 p.m., https://twitter.com/jdgreear/status/992842255387029504.

56. Jon Harris, *Social Justice Goes To Church: The New Left in Modern American Evangelicalism* (Ambassador International, 2020), 165-167.

57. David Platt, *Before You Vote* (Freely Give Company, 2020), 42; John Piper, *Could a Pastor At Bethlehem Have Voted for Obama?*, *Desiring God*, April 17, 2010, https://www.desiringgod.org/interviews/could-a-pastor-at-bethlehem-have-voted-for-obama.

58. Arthur Melzer, "The Origin of the Counter-Enlightenment: Rousseau and the New Religion of Sincerity," *The American Political Science Review* 90, no. 2 (June 1996): 345, 352, 354-355.

59. Herbert Marcuse, *Philosophy, Psychoanalysis and Emancipation: Collected Papers of Herbert Marcuse Volume Five*, (Routledge, 2010), 184-188.

ical protest and reaffirm the conservative values on which the white middle class's traditional illusions of superiority are grounded." Nevertheless, he also saw how a "new interpretation of Christianity" could lead to "enlightenment" instead of "pacification."[60] Simply put, some of the major framers of today's social justice theory envisioned a modified Christianity centered on mankind and advancing immediate social change.

The Sources of Evil and Contentment

However, for orthodox Christians, the problems in the world are ultimately internal and not external. Even if it were possible to eliminate every institution accused of injustice, it would still not result in a just world. Jesus taught that the things that "defile a man" come "out of the heart," including "evil thoughts, murders, adulteries, fornications, thefts, false witness, [and] slanders."[61] Scripture repeatedly says that people are spiritually enslaved to sin in their natural state.[62] It even teaches that creation is under a curse and longs for restoration as the result of sin.[63] This does not mean everything is as it should be according to God's original design. King Solomon wrote that "God made men upright, but they have sought out many devices."[64] But it does mean that Christianity, and the political conservatism it helped inspire, are right to be skeptical of concentrated power, untested human innovations, and the instant demolition of stabilizing social institutions. Mankind gravitates toward chaos and corruption, not utopia.

Many social justice advocates, on the other hand, believe imposing ideological equality will not only help overcome inequalities resulting from sin and preference, but also disparities fundamental to creation itself. Justice means forcibly eradicating social differences between men and women, expanding human rights to animals, and reducing parental influence over children. The list of injustices increases on a daily basis as activists discover new inequities. This rebellion against creation design and natural order stands

---

60. Derrick Bell, *The Derrick Bell Reader*, ed. Richard Delgado and Jean Stefancic, Critical America (NYU Press, 2005), 188, 82.

61. Matt 15:17-19

62. John 8:34; Rom 6:16; 2 Peter 2:19

63. Gen 3:16-19; Rom 5:12; 8:19-23

64. Eccl 7:29; Luke 10:27; Eph 6:9

in stark contrast to the generally accepted view throughout history that justice takes into account both ingrained and inevitable hierarchies.

Though many consider his ideas offensive today, Aristotle thought that "the relation of male to female is by nature a relation of superior to inferior and ruler to ruled." He also observed that excessive immigration caused a "dissimilarity of stock" that produced "conflict." The ancient Greek philosopher even famously called some men "slaves by nature" who possessed reduced mental capabilities and benefitted from the directions and limitations imposed by others.[65] Aristotle was not unique in his opinions. Most societies throughout history recognized similar differences and acknowledged them in their judicial arrangements. Interestingly, general social attitudes toward women, slaves, unwanted children, and other commonly mistreated groups changed as Christianity gained influence.

For example, Roman slavery did not include many of the protections found in the Mosaic law. Slaves did not have rights. They could not have a "real family" legally. Civil punishment for crime was generally more severe for them that it was for freemen. Kidnaping to obtain slaves was not uncommon, and masters could kill, rape, and use them for prostitution with social approval.[66] However, early Christian teaching forbade kidnaping, granted slaves membership in the church, and instructed masters to "give up threatening" while treating them with "justice and fairness."[67] Christians also rescued infanticide victims and charitably gave to provide for orphans, widows, and the poor among them. Their recognition of intrinsic worth and purpose for women, practice of marital fidelity, and teaching that husbands should love their wives sacrificially marked a departure from Roman assumptions.[68] Over

---

65. Aristotle, *The Politics* (University of Chicago Press, 2010), 40-41, 152.

66. Coby Evans, *Roman Slavery: The Everyday Lives of Average Citizens and Slaves* (Self Publisher, 2019), loc 315, 373, 444, 634-638, Kindle; Scott Bartchy, *First-Century Slavery and the Interpretation of 1 Corinthians 7:21* (Wipf and Stock Publishers, 2003), 38-39, 45-46.

67. 1 Tim 1:10; Phil 1:17; Burton Scott Easton, ed., *The Apostolic Tradition of Hippolytus* (Cambridge University Press, 2014), 41; Eph 6:9; Col 4:1 Philip Schaff, *The Teaching of the Twelve Apostles* (Funk & Wagnalls, 1889), 178.

68. Acts 6:1; Eph 5:25; Margaret Dunlop Gibson, *The Didascalia Apostolorum in English* (C.J. Clay, 1903), 81; P. Gardner-Smith and F. J. Foakes-Jackson, *The Christian Religion* (Cambridge University Press, 2014), 48; John Bagnell Bury, *A History of the Later Roman Empire: From Arcadius to Irene (395 A.D. to 800 A.D.)* (Macmillan and Company, 1889),

time, Christian ethics filtered into law and provided the basis for much of Western civilization.

During this transition, Christians generally did not embrace immediate coercion by starting a revolution or provoking a war. Neither did they blame Rome's history of colonialism and systemic oppression on its paganism and decadence. They did not destroy statues of famous Romans or burn the capitol to the ground despite Nero's accusation they did. Instead, they acted as though the human heart was the ultimate source of evil and worked through the existing channels available to reform Rome from the bottom up. This civilizational shift arose not from enforcing abstract equality but from embracing the Creator's law, order, and love that offered divine purpose and human dignity.

Christians know that social perfection in this temporary life is not possible. Even in the best justice system, some crimes will still go unpunished until God judges all people in the life to come. However, the Bible assumes that true contentment this side of heaven is possible. Christians live with an understanding that justice means they deserve divine punishment for breaking God's law in both word and deed.[69] Yet, instead of giving them justice, Scripture teaches that God gave them mercy "because of His great love" demonstrated through Christ's death on behalf of all who put their trust in Him.[70] Living with a sense of forgiveness, divine purpose, and looking for opportunities to love God and others is a recipe for joy even in the most challenging circumstances.[71]

The famous Olympic gold medalist Eric Liddell is held up as an example of someone marked by this spirit of joy. Yet as a missionary in China, he faced floods, robbers, war, risked his life numerous times, ended up being separated from his wife for over half of their marriage, was overworked, was often taken for granted, and eventually died from a brain tumor that would have been avoidable had he not been a prisoner in a Japanese war camp during the second world war. One time a friend asked if he regretted giving his life on the mission field. Liddell replied, "I have more joy and

---

20; Carroll Osburn, *Essays on Women in Earliest Christianity*, Volume 2 (Wipf and Stock Publishers, 2007), 378.

69. 1 Sam 16:7; Rev 21:8

70. Eph 2:4, Rom 5:8

71. Psalm 35:9; Rom 12:12; 2 Cor 12:10; Phil 2:17; 4:11-13; Heb 12:2; James 1:2-4

freedom in the work than I have ever experienced before." This is because Liddell did not obsess over his present circumstances. Instead, he accepted them and looked for a higher purpose in them. In his book *Disciplines of the Christian Life*, Liddell explained that his "greatest joy [was] just to do what pleases [Jesus]."[72]

David Michell, a young boy in the Weihsien prison camp where Liddell died, wrote about the way he conducted himself in such atrocious conditions:

> He lived in the very crowded men's dormitory near us (each man had a space of only three by six feet) and supervised our daily rollcall when the guards came to count us. One day a week 'Uncle Eric' would look after us, giving our teachers a break. His gentle face and warm smile, even as he taught us games with the limited equipment available, showed us how much he loved children and how much he missed his own.[73]

Liddell loved God and others. His favorite hymn, which he taught the prisoners, was the old German song "Be Still My Soul." The first verse says:

> *Be still, my soul: the Lord is on thy side;*
> *Bear patiently the cross of grief or pain;*
> *Leave to thy God to order and provide;*
> *In every change he faithful will remain.*
> *Be still, my soul: thy best, thy heavenly friend*
> *Through thorny ways leads to a joyful end.*

On Wednesday February 21, 1945, a malnourished, once-great-athlete, greatly weakened and dying, pushed himself to walk around the Weihsien prison camp. One observer later said, "as usual he was smiling." That evening, as he lay in bed giving a discipleship lesson, Liddell underwent a series of three strokes that lead to his death. His last words were said to be, "It's complete surrender." In his pocket a note was found with the line: "All will

---

72. Eric Liddell, *The Disciplines of the Christian Life* (Nashville : Abingdon Press, 1985), 78.

73. David Michell, "Dr. David J Michell," *Eric Liddell Centre* (blog), March 12, 2017, https://www.ericliddell.org/dr-david-j-michell/.

be well." Liddell's example, like millions of Christians throughout history, is a testimony to how beautiful life can truly be even when hardship and injustice prevail.[74]

The social justice movement is not satisfied and never can be since abuse, oppression, and disparities will always exist in the temporal realm. The created order, social hierarchies, and human sin will continue until the consummation of all things. While most true Christians do strive to love their neighbors by upholding God's law, engaging in charity, and even using force to defend others, they are not under the illusion that their mission on earth is to create utopia, especially through dismantling order and design.

In John 10:10, Jesus said, "The thief comes only to steal and kill and destroy; I came that they may have life, and have it abundantly." Christ offers joy in this life and eternal joy in the sinless world to come. Social justice offers what it has delivered every time it is tried: jealousy, envy, bitterness, destruction, corruption, tyranny, and ultimately, civil slavery to an impersonal, centralized bureaucracy. At this crucial moment, it is up to evangelicals, and Americans in general, to decide which path to follow.

74. Duncan Hamilton, *For the Glory: The Untold and Inspiring Story of Eric Liddell, Hero of Chariots of Fire* (Penguin Random House LLC, 2017); 212, 323-324, 337.

WOKE EVANGELICAL TACTICS

August 6, 2021

Anyone paying close attention to how social justice activists convince evangelical Christians to adopt their principles notices four general tactics:

1. Associate egalitarianism and activism with the gospel.
2. Attach "quality-of-life" issues to the "pro-life" movement.
3. Assume conservative views conflict with public witness.
4. Attribute worldly motives to conservative causes.

In some ways, influential evangelicals out-of-step with the people they claim to serve, picked up where the "new atheists" of more than a decade ago left off. They present Christianity in general, and the church in particular, as responsible or complicit in past and present bigotries. Western colonialism, American slavery, barriers for women, the holocaust, opposition to immigration, an unbridled free-market, racial segregation, and the persecution of LGBTQ+ people are all placed on the doorstep of the church. Only, instead of coming to the new atheist's conclusion that Christianity is evil, evangelical elites blame these social maladies on an inauthentic version of Christianity they separate themselves from.

This strategy has proven effective in convincing Christians to feel ashamed of their own history. In some cases, professing evangelicals, desperate to find a link between egalitarian heroes and their own tradition, even claim heretics of the past as their own. In other cases, this thinking leads to a crisis-of-faith. How can Christianity be true if its practitioners for hundreds of years promoted evil? Of course, this posture plays right into the hands of Marxist academics working toward revolution for decades by vilifying their own countries. In an ever-widening list of abuses, whether true or manufactured, Christians are forced to feel the weight of their involvement in oppression.

I remember a few years ago when a fellow seminary student suggested in class that Christians should apologize for their complicity in the holocaust. The professor responded by saying that he believed more and more evangelicals were coming to the same conclusion and that it was a positive development. Instead, I suggested Christians should become more involved in teaching their people about the truths and complexities of history so they would not be easily persuaded by ideological oversimplifications intended to evoke misplaced guilt. My comment was not accepted favorably, but I still stand by it—and more so now than I did then. While it may be true that Christians are capable of evil, it is not true that it characterizes them.

Even a cursory look at many of the social ills attributed to Christianity, shows major gaps in the current narratives. For example, it was not orthodox Lutheran doctrine so much as it was the waning influence of it in favor of higher criticism and neo-orthodoxy that allowed for the scientific racism that led to the holocaust. And while there were Christians who incorrectly favored forced racial segregation in the United States, for many the civil rights movement was a peripheral campaign associated with things like ecumenicism, Soviet subversion, and disrespect for law and order. Also, Christians who oppose importing large groups of unassimilated migrants claim their motive is not hating others, but rather loving their own neighbors and wanting to preserve the valuable things about their culture for future generations.

Underlying much of this criticism is an assumption that Christians had the influence and understanding necessary to stop great evil and refused to do it. Yet failing to participate in the overturning of established hierarchies attached to the created order is not evil. Neither is undermining sinful habits by working through conventional channels instead of revolutionary ones. Occasionally, even social justice advocates can see the truth in this.

For instance, if Oskar Schindler staged a protest in Berlin during the holocaust he would likely have been executed or held as a political prisoner. Instead, he engaged in racially-based slavery by purchasing kidnaped Jews from the Nazis. Yet his participation in an unjust system was intended to save lives. Unlike consistent ideologues who view most every issue through the prism of a moral binary, Christians understand many issues are decided through wisely applying absolute principles to various situations. Living within the boundaries of an evil arrangement does not necessarily make one guilty of that evil. This is why Paul instructed masters, in a Roman slave system attached to much evil, to apply God's law themselves. Things like paying taxes (some of which go to Planned Parenthood), shopping at Apple (which uses sweatshop labor), and working in the welfare system (the Bible forbids rewarding someone with food who refuses to work) are not sins even if the related organizations need reform.

Modern evangelical elites accept the political left's shortlist of social crimes, fail to consider their prevalence in non-Western societies, and then blame their own religion for the sin of not participating in enough activism and revolutionary activity. However, the worst part of all is the next step. Influential evangelicals also confuse faithfulness to the gospel with egalitarian ethics and social activism. Russell Moore thinks it is a "gospel issue" to allow illegal migrants to use services paid for by American taxes without objection. *Christianity Today* recently published an article about the Me Too movement in which the author states that "the gospel of Jesus Christ requires us to believe the word of women." Of course, the examples are endless. If someone strongly resists the "equity, diversity, and inclusion" agenda, they are cast to the outer darkness reserved for idolaters, Pharisees, and certainly not respectable Christians.

Another tactic of social justice evangelicals is to attach "quality-of-life" issues to the "pro-life" movement. Because evangelicals have a strong tradition of opposing abortion it is very difficult to convince them using the standard secular pro-abortion arguments. Instead, political progressives try to hijack the movement by adding social justice concerns and treating them as if they are just as important as breaking God's direct command not to murder. Things like systemic racism, environmental issues, and even personal decisions like smoking are considered pro-life issues.

Ron Sider, in his 1987 book "Completely Pro-Life," was one of the first to make this argument to evangelicals. Sider defined being "completely pro-life" as "defend[ing] human life wherever it is threatened." That is how he could go after pro-life Senator Jesse Helms for inconsistency since he opposed abortion but also supported government subsidies for tobacco. The mistake in this thinking is comparing something like smoking, a quality-of-life choice made by adults who probably also eat cheeseburgers and fail to exercise at times, with actual murder. The unlawful taking of another person's life is very different than choosing to drink soda. One is a sin in and of itself and subject to civil penalty in God's law. The other could potentially be negligent, but it is an issue of personal jurisdiction and does not usually accompany an intent to immediately end one's life.

Over the last few years, things like police brutality and following government guidelines concerning the Covid outbreak are being attached to the "pro-life" cause. *The Gospel Coalition* published an article about NFL player Benjamin Watson's pro-life work, which included the problem of police brutality against black people. Popular evangelical author Karen Swallow Prior believes "'pro-life' Christians" brought "the culture of death" they warned others about because they failed to follow Covid "health protocols." This new interpretation of a "womb-to-tomb" pro-life position is changing the movement from within.

Allegedly contributing to increased numbers of Covid cases by attending a church service, not wearing a mask, or declining a vaccine are not the same as actively and intentionally murdering someone with the permission of the government. Likewise, police brutality does not enjoy the sanction of law, whereas abortion does. Given the size of the United States and the corruption existing in the heart of mankind, it should come as no surprise that some police departments cover up incidents in which officers murder innocent people. This is very different than a hypothetical Supreme Court case granting departments this ability with impunity.

The concern many conservative Christians have about the holistic pro-life approach is that, instead of strengthening opposition to legalized abortion, it deludes opposition. That is how evangelical leaders like Richard Mouw and Joel Hunter were able to support "Pro-Life Evangelicals for Biden." Things like racism, poverty, healthcare, smoking, climate change, minimum wage, and affordable access to childcare were all life issues considered, in the balance, more important than Donald Trump's anti-abortion policies. Such thinking seems like it comes from a severely broken sense of proportion, but for many young pro-life evangelicals, it is starting to work.

Another tactic used to neutralize politically conservative viewpoints within evangelicalism is to portray them as in conflict with a Christian commitment to be a public witness. In other words, "What will the people we are trying to reach with our message think if they find out you support a conservative cause?" Consider these titles from *The Gospel Coalition*: "Be Winsome and Persuasive," "Blog Winsomely," "Trading Moral Outrage for Winsome Persuasion," and "Al Mohler on Confronting the Culture Winsomely Yet Subversively."

What one finds when they look at these pieces is that an unfavorable perception exists within evangelicalism about itself. Christian leaders think their followers have a problem being rude, unfriendly, rigid, and hateful. They also tend to lack love, compassion, and gospel-centeredness. The truth is, this side of heaven Christians will never be perfect and many of these charges do apply in certain situations. But is this attitude unique or characteristic of Christianity? It is important to remember that in the face of political movements forcing evil agendas there is a place for anger and uncompromising fortitude.

David certainly did not approach Goliath in a "winsome way." Rather, he declared: "Who is this uncircumcised Philistine, that he should taunt the armies of the living God?" Neither was Elijah winsome when he mocked the prophets of Baal. John the Baptist called King Herod a fox. Jesus very said the Pharisees were "whitewashed tombs which on the outside appear beautiful, but inside they are full of dead men's bones and all uncleanness." Paul expressed his desire for false teachers to "mutilate themselves." The Bible is filled with examples of men who were not very winsome and would definitely be considered angry today. Yet Scripture teaches that while there is never a time to sin, there is a time to be angry about sin. Righteous indignation is sometimes appropriate.

One of the more recent popular catchphrases used by evangelical elites over the past decade is the term "cultural engagement." Trevin Wax, who works for the North American Mission Board and Wheaton College, sees the term as including "understand[ing] people and cultures," "present[ing] the gospel as a 'better story' than the false hopes of the world," and "creat[ing]… a new culture." Often, it seems the phrase conveys an almost obsession with understanding how modern people think and their preferences so as to effectively persuade them toward Christianity. The assumption seems to be that Christians are on the outside of culture and need to strategically manufacture a culture of their own capable of competing with the outside culture and drawing outsiders in the least offensive way possible. This is the history of neo-evangelicalism over the past several decades. In order to keep up with the times, evangelical industries reinvent themselves almost every 10 years. Yet nowhere is this thinking represented in Scripture.

Though Christians are to be separate from the world ("the lust of the flesh and the lust of the eyes and the boastful pride of life"), they are necessarily embedded within the culture they are members of and should understand enough about themselves and the people around them to be an effective witness. It is true that there were times when the Apostle Paul was around Jewish people and willingly lived by standards in the Jewish law for the sake of the gospel. Yet his goal was to keep from unnecessarily offending them, not creating an alternative culture to attract them.

The last major way that social justice advocates are pushing evangelicals toward the left is by attributing worldly motives to conservative candidates or causes. I remember as a student at Southeastern Baptist Theological Seminary hearing professor Bruce Ashford in chapel characterize the political right as idolizing the "ethno-nation" to the point of being "unjust toward people" who are not members. Tim Keller regularly compares political conservatism to idolatry or false religion. *The Gospel Coalition* published a blog a few years ago entitled: "The Selfishness of the Religious Right." Many evangelical leaders ascribed the motive of gaining and keeping power to "Christian nationalists" and Trump voters over the past few years. To give one example: Beth Moore recently said that "wedding evangelicalism to a political party... was also about power. Position. Access."

In a sense, evangelicals are probably somewhat mimicking the narrative emanating from left-wing media voices. MSNBC host Joe Scarborough said that "Fear of Trump and lust for Power have made cowards of GOP politicians and evangelical leaders." CNN recently published an article claiming that "evangelicals traded their radicalism for social acceptance and political power."

Of course, power in itself is not necessarily a bad thing. In fact, God delegates power to the government for a reason. If the government's job, according to Romans 13, is to be "a minister of God to you for good," then it makes sense that Christians, who know what God says is "good," would want to gain and use political power as salt and light. Compared to the history of the world, Christians in the United States have a unique opportunity to express their convictions through voting. The way in which political power is gained and used can be evil, but power in itself is ordained by God.

There is no doubt that there are evil people after personal power on the political right. But treating this fact as if it characterizes all political conservatives is inconsistent. Evangelical elites do not say all members of the political left support progressive candidates because they want perversion, stealing, and murder. Yet the Bible describes many of their fundamental objectives this way. Perhaps if today's evangelical elites said such things they would not be winsome?

The overall effect of associating egalitarianism and activism with the gospel, attaching "quality-of-life" issues to the "pro-life" movement, assuming conservative views conflict with public witness, and attributing worldly motives to conservative causes has been to move evangelicals toward the left politically. If evangelicals are not careful, their new inconsistent ethical views will bleed into their core theology over time. They will no longer be evangelicals. Some, including this author, already thinks this is taking place except for one thing—many of the people in the pews are still resistant to these changes. While those running evangelical organizations may be going in a bad direction, the gap between them and those they are supposed to serve is fairly wide. It is up to small town pastors and faithful laymen and laywomen to uphold biblical thinking and reject the social justice movement while there is still time.

APPENDIX 2

DAVID FRENCH AND INTERGENERATIONAL SIN

July 26, 2021

David French, a senior editor for *The Dispatch*, recently appealed to biblical texts in 2 Samuel, 2 Kings, Daniel, Nehemiah, and Leviticus in order to defend the view that modern American Christians are complicit in "structural racism" and possess an "intergenerational obligation to remedy historic injustice." In 2 Samuel 21, God caused a famine in Israel in reaction to King Saul's previous attempt to break Israel's treaty with the Gibeonites and exterminate them instead of simply treating them as "slaves."[1] As a result, Saul's successor King David handed over seven of Saul's sons and grandsons to be punished for the sin of "Saul and his bloody house." French asserts: "Saul was king before David, and God was punishing Israel years after Saul's regime because of Saul's sin. It was the next king, David's, responsibility to make things right." He concludes that "Israel remained responsible for its former leader's sins, and they were required to make amends." This responsibility extends to "the United States of America," which he believes fails "to ameliorate the effects of slavery and Jim Crow... embedded in our system."[2]

However, it is significant that civil justice was limited only to living members of Saul's "bloody house" and did not extend to David's sons or

1. 2 Sam 21:1-14; Josh 9:15, 23

2. David French, "Structural Racism Isn't Wokeness, It's Reality," July 25, 2021, https://frenchpress.thedispatch.com/p/structural-racism-isnt-wokeness-its.

132

any other Israelite. It is also obvious the situation was unique and not normative. David was unaware of how to rectify the circumstance from God's law. Likewise, the Gibeonites were not interested in reparations or violating Israel's due process by putting anyone to death.[3] The passage does not clarify whether God approved of David's actions. But the final result did ensure that Samuel's prophecy, that Saul's kingdom would not endure, came to pass.[4] Interestingly, "God was moved by prayer for the land," not after the executions, but rather after the bones of Saul, Jonathan, and the seven executed sons were buried in their family grave.

Most biblical interpretation textbooks advise studying concepts in difficult passages by first understanding passages that are easy to understand on the same subject. Ezekiel 18 states that a son who "has practiced justice and righteousness" shall live, but the "person who sins will die." It is unequivocally clear, according to verse 20 that "the son will not bear the punishment for the father's iniquity, nor will the father bear the punishment for the son's iniquity." Instead, each person will answer for their own actions. This does not mean that children cannot learn and repeat the sinful habits of their parents. But it does mean that when they are punished for participating in the sins of their ancestors, it is because they are actually participating, not because they inherit someone else's guilt.

French uses the way Josiah, Daniel, and the Israelites during Moses' and Nehemiah's times confessed their father's sins as evidence that modern Americans must repent and atone for "systemic racism."[5] Yet in all these examples, the current generation was actually confessing sins in which they themselves were participating as they continued to perpetuate the sinful patterns of their parents. Perhaps this behavior makes even more sense in the context of a national covenant between God and Israel.

It is common for social justice activists to oppose the idea that America is, like Israel, a "chosen" nation. Neither do they believe the civil laws specific to Israel apply to modern liberal democracies. For example, David French believes Drag Queen Story Hours at public libraries are "one of the blessings

---

3. Num 39:6-34

4. 1 Sam 13:14

5. 2 Kings 22:13; Dan 9:16; Lev 26:40; Neh 9:2

of liberty" and opposes efforts to limit their access to the public square.[6] This is out of step with Deuteronomy 22:5, which states: "A woman shall not wear man's clothing, nor shall a man put on a woman's clothing; for whoever does these things is an abomination to the Lord your God." Yet French has no problem stretching and selectively citing unique examples from the Old Testament he can use to bolster his arguments for systemic racism.

6. Condé Nast, "David French, Sohrab Ahmari, and the Battle for the Future of Conservatism," *The New Yorker*, September 12, 2019, https://www.newyorker.com/news/the-political-scene/david-french-sohrab-ahmari-and-the-battle-for-the-future-of-conservatism.

APPENDIX 3
TIME TO CANCEL LOTTIE MOON

June 23, 2020

Note: This is written as a parody to help Southern Baptists see how the logic imposed on them by social justice advocates in their denomination, if taken to its logical conclusion, could lead to what the article describes.

IT IS NO secret that Southern Baptist leaders carry a large burden of white guilt for historic situations and symbols they consider insensitive to Americans blessed with African lineage. They are especially ashamed of their own denomination's history. And, interestingly, they think they somehow have the power to change the legacy of their self-assessed complicity through lamentation and other measures (a very "white" assumption from the perspective of critical race theory advocates, if there ever was one).

In 1989, the Convention issued a statement against racism and bigotry. They apologized for slavery in 1995. In 1996, they made a statement condemning arson in African American churches. In 2007, they denounced the Dred Scott Decision. In 2015, there was another statement on racial reconciliation. The next year, they issued a statement against the Confederate Battle Flag. In 2017, the Convention adopted a resolution against "Alt-Right White Supremacy."

In 2018, Danny Akin, the president of Southeastern Baptist Theological Seminary sponsored a resolution which, among other things, condemned the first president of the convention, William B. Johnson for promoting slavery in his inaugural address. Johnson's crime concerned his disagreement with the Mission Board in Boston, which "had placed itself in direct opposition to the Constitution of the Convention" by disqualifying slave-holders from becoming missionaries and had "failed to prove—That slavery is, in all circumstances, sinful." This resolution failed amidst the crowded slate of resolutions also condemning some form of, you guessed it, racism.

The Convention instead adopted a resolution against using the "Curse of Ham" as a justification for slavery and another statement condemning racism. Add to this the various statements written, sponsored, or supported by Southern Baptist entities and one begins to swim in a sea of anti-racist statements all attempting to once-and-for-all rid the Convention of, as Al Mohler likes to call it, "the stain of racism."

The latest attempt to use racial animosity as a pretext for societal revolution affords Southern Baptists yet another opportunity to condemn one of their most cherished subjects—racism. Prominent SBC pastors like Thabiti Anywabile and David Platt encouraged marching with Black Lives Matter. The president of the Convention, J.D. Greear, called for the retirement of the "Broadus gavel"—deemed unholy for having been the unfortunate block of wood to have been in contact early on with a slave-holder and Confederate supporter. The Mississippi Baptist Convention took it upon themselves this week to condemn the Mississippi State Flag for its symbolic Confederate imagery.

As advocates of cheap bravery rush to show solidarity with the forces of revolution and obtain their unearned "pat on the head" from media elites, one wonders, where this will all end? Perhaps Southern Baptist comrades should showcase their fidelity to the revolution by demonstrating some, you know, REAL sacrifice. It will be easy for the scoffers and "exvangelicals" to see through token measures meant to placate other comrades. However, what if the SBC were to make a financial sacrifice for their oppressed minority brothers and sisters made in the image of God? What if Southern Baptists eliminated the Lottie Moon offering for the racism it is!

Think about it. Lottie Moon was born into a "fifteen-hundred-acre tobacco plantation." Her father "was the largest slaveholder (fifty-two slaves) in Albemarle County" Virginia.[1] Lottie never, that we know of, apologized

---

1. "Lottie Moon," Deer Creek Church (blog), accessed August 6, 2021, https://deercreekchurch.net/lottie-moon/.

for her privilege or her family's complicity in holding slaves. In 1875, Lottie Moon said, "Where the Caucasian goes, he carries energy and an inferior race is aroused by the contact."[2] In 1876, Moon claimed that "self-respect" compelled her to reject any potential "decision of any Chinaman or body of Chinamen" to determine the place of her ministry. She likened such an affront to an "African church in Richmond" telling Dr. Warren where he could live.[3] Moon was most likely referring to Dr. Edward Warren, who had been the medical inspector of the Army of Northern Virginia. Lottie Moon's sister, Oriana Russell Moon Andrews, had served the Confederate Army as a nurse under Warren.[4]

Also in 1876, Moon talked about another missionary, Mrs. Holmes, who did not want to move and abandon her "duty to these poor heathen," but knew her son Landrum needed to go to the United States. The boy would likely live with Methodist relatives "Northern in political sentiment," an arrangement whose influence Holmes was "not willing to subject her boy to." Moon sought alternative arrangements for the boy to help him avoid what to her was an understandably negative situation.[5]

In addition, Moon said Chinese funeral processions contained "barbaric pomp and show" in 1884.[6] Two years later she proclaimed concerning China, "The life here as we Western people consider life, is exceedingly narrow & contracted. Constant contact with people of a low civilization & many disgusting habits is a trial to one of refined feelings & tastes."[7] In 1907, Moon opined that a large "Reunion of Confederate veterans" must have been "pleasant."[8]

This cursory sketch of some of Lottie Moon's views make it clear that if Southern Baptists want to truly show their loyalty to the spirit of the age, they will disband the Lottie Moon Christmas offering. As an added bonus,

2. "Lottie Moon to Henry A. Tupper," March 13, 1875.

3. Lottie Moon, *Send the Light: Lottie Moon's Letters and Other Writings* (Mercer University Press, 2002), 162.

4. Jennifer Davis McDaid, "Oriana Russell Moon Andrews (1834–1883)," *Dictionary of Virginia Biography*, Library of Virginia, 2016.

5. Moon, *Send the Light*, 35.

6. "Lottie Moon to Foreign Mission Journal," August 1, 1884.

7. "Lottie Moon to Foreign Mission Journal," December 13, 1886.

8. Moon, *Send the Light*, 425.

perhaps they should return $1.5 billion in funds collected in support for their colonization work they refer to as "missions." Western male Christians, exploiting the legacy of a "racist" white female, have tried to dominate the minds of brown-skinned members of minority religions for far too long.

Mr. Greear, tear down your idol. Cancel Lottie Moon.

APPENDIX 4
ON THE DECONSTRUCTION OF JOSHUA HARRIS

August 2, 2019

As many in the Christian community are well aware, Joshua Harris, author of *I Kissed Dating Goodbye*, has left the faith recently, stating: "By all the measurements that I have for defining a Christian, I am not a Christian." This development has caused many to seriously question how someone so seemingly grounded could walk away from everything they once believed. After all, not all of us have seven Christian book titles with our names on them.

Of course, both Christ and the Apostles predicted this scenario. Judas himself was able to keep the other eleven apostles from suspecting his own apostasy. But there were clues along the way. For Judas, it was his greed. For Josh Harris, it's something else.

Michael Farris, who knew Harris personally, recently wrote in an open letter to him: "You thought your faith and your marriage were based on formulas. They never went deeper than that." He added: "You haven't walked away from a relationship with Jesus. You have walked away from the culture you were raised in." To someone who has read many of Josh's books, this sounds like a fair assessment. Whether it's *I Kissed Dating Goodbye*, or *Why Church Matters*, Josh always wrote very pragmatically. This does not necessarily have to be bad thing, unless of course, it's the only thing.

In 2017, Josh publicly showed signs of rethinking his religious views in a Ted X talk entitled, "Strong Enough to Be Wrong," in which he stated that "being wrong" about courtship "affected his own sense of identity." People don't usually say such things about formulas unless those formulas are necessarily tied to core beliefs.

Harris's attempt at humility was actually a self-focused revelation of his own pride. An inflated view of his own influence caused him to take responsibility for even failed relationships resulting from a misapplication of his book. For example, Harris writes in *I Kissed Dating Goodbye*: "Without purity, God's gift of sexuality becomes a dangerous game." In *Boy Meets Girl*, he gives an example of two previously married individuals pursuing purity together. However, in the 2018 documentary, "I Survived I Kissed Dating Goodbye," Harris mistakenly takes responsibility for those who wrongfully equated purity with virginity—something he did not do in his writings. Even the falling marriage rate in the church is somehow blamed on Harris's "purity culture."

Like a mathematician with the wrong result, Harris dissects his alleged formula:

Marriage = Sex = Fulfillment

The take away? Purity culture propagated the lie that marriage would offer fulfillment and it didn't. Marriage was an "idol."

It is at this point that we should recognize a similar talking point emanating from the social justice flavor of American Christianity. Russell Moore says, "dark powers would have us idolize ourselves or by extension our families." Matt Trexler and Sammy Rhodes, two "same-sex attracted" Christians, talk about the church's "tendency to idolize marriage." Carolyn McCulley, Jennifer Marshall, and Betsy Childs Howard, believe there has been an "idolization of marriage." Elizabeth Woodson wants to "dethrone our idol of marriage." Tim Keller asserts that "traditional religion has often made an idol out of the family."

Josh Harris's denouncement of his own book, and by extension purity culture, did not happen in a vacuum. At the very moment culture is deconstructing creation norms, leaders in the church are also minimizing or tossing them aside. Josh Harris just took it one step further. Josh describes his own kissing Christianity goodbye as "deconstruction," stating: "To the LGBTQ+ community, I want to say that I am sorry for the views that I taught in my books and as a pastor regarding sexuality. I regret standing against marriage equality, for not affirming you and your place in the church, and for any ways that my writing and speaking contributed to a culture of exclusion and bigotry."

In the documentary, Harris focuses on "asking questions" and having "conversations" along his "personal journey." He concludes toward the end, "life is full of contradictions." The postmodern assumptions Josh may have picked up at Regent College, are alive and well in popular evangelicalism. They fuel the social justice movement: the last stop before complete apostasy. In the words of J. Gresham Machan, "The chief modern rival of Christianity is 'liberalism.' An examination of the teachings of liberalism in comparison with those of Christianity will show that at every point the two movements are in direct opposition." Unlike many Christian leaders who push social justice, at least Josh Harris is honest enough to admit what he's doing.

SOUTH AFRICA IS TEACHING US A LESSON, WILL WE LEARN?

June 10, 2021

Last night I decided to watch Laura Southern's "Farmlands" (2018) documentary about the ongoing proto-genocide against white South Africans, especially farmers. Both the South African government and the media continue to suppress information exposing this reality. Perhaps watching this documentary as an American in 2021 hits closer to home than it would have had I seen it when it first came out. The parallels between what is happening in South Africa and what is happening in the United States are striking.

Though Southern does not highlight everything that led to the crisis at hand, anyone with a cursory knowledge of South African politics knows that preceding and accompanying much of the current violence has been a campaign to destroy and rewrite South African history. Not only are older books on South African history destroyed and replaced with Marxist retellings, but geographic locations have been renamed and monuments to white South Africans taken down. Sound familiar?

Like the United States, South Africa has a history of racial tension famously manifested in apartheid. Also like the United States, Marxists exploit this fact without giving a full account of what preceded apartheid and what took place after the African National Congress (ANC) took control of the country.

In 1652, the Dutch East Indian Company settled South African's western coast while the rest of the country was inhabited by the nomadic Khoisan people. The Dutch maintained primarily peaceful relationships with the Khoisan by purchasing land, trading, and even marrying in some cases as they expanded into the interior of the region. Like the United States, many of the original settlers were indentured servants and lived under economic hardship as they cultivated their new home. The Trekboer and Voortrekkers were frontiersmen who settled north beyond the Dutch colony and are known today as Afrikaners with their own language and culture.

As the Voortrekkers entered the area, Bantu tribes who lived to their north were at war. Shaka, the king of the Zulu tribe, defeated most of the other tribes, but it did not result in stability. In 1823, a rebellion resulted in the deaths of between one and two million people, leaving the area almost completely depopulated. Several of the tribes fled south toward the Voortrekkers. Their sudden arrival created tension and signaled a new more violent relationship between the Dutch settlers and Bantu tribes.

In 1838, Zulu king Dingane heinously beat Voortrek leader Piet Retief and 100 of his men in a surprise attack disguised as a friendly gathering. They then destroyed his entire camp including women, children, and Khoisan people who lived with the Voortrekkers in what became known as the Weenen massacre.

The Union of South Africa formed in 1910 after the British defeated the Dutch farmers (Boer). Though separation between blacks and whites was a social convention, it eventually became law after the election of the National Party in 1948 which banned interracial marriages, promoted racial registration, and relocated many of the Bantu tribes to their tribal homelands.

In 1961, Nelson Mandela, a member of the South African Communist Party, helped found the Spear of the Nation, which was a forerunner to today's African National Congress. They announced their existence with 57 bombings in one day. As Mandela served his 27-year prison sentence, the anti-apartheid movement became even more radical as cruel and unusual methods, like necklacing, became popular to punish even black people who were thought to be collaborating with the government.

In the 1970s and 80s, internal and external pressure caused instability in the country. Eventually the National Party negotiated with the African National Congress to end apartheid in 1991. In 1994, Mandela became president. In 1996, the government legalized abortion and adopted a new constitution emphasizing positive rights, such as the right to education and a universal basic income. In 2000, firearm ownership was restricted. In 2003, The Broad-Based Black Economic Empowerment Act attempted to compensate black people for being victims during a history of systemic racism by regulating private hiring policies. The South African Preferential Procurement Regulations further regulate government industries and government contracts by adjusting for racial victimhood. Same-sex marriage became legal in 2006.

Though the similarities are not exact, the position of the Dutch in South Africa bears a striking resemblance to the American situation. Not only did European settlers in the present-day United States clash with tribal peoples on the frontier, but they also struggled against the British, resettled tribal peoples and experienced civil unrest during times of racial integration. Though the political establishments in both countries envisioned peaceful race relations after altering legal policies in order to foster integration, in both countries these dreams have been temporary at best.

The present-day Black Lives Matter movement echoes the policies and attitudes of South African political groups like the African National Congress, Black First Land First, and the Economic Freedom Fighters who are known for calling for the deaths of white farmers at their rallies. "The Land Issue" has become a major source of controversy over the past few years. A rising tide of murders of rural white farmers has been accompanied by a political narrative calling for the redistribution of white-owned farms.

Between 2012 and 2016 the attacks on farms increased 72.9% according to the Blood Sisters, a private organization responsible for cleaning up crime scenes. These statistics are both undocumented and unreported by the government and news organizations. "We Can Stop the Genocide," a group advocating for rural white farmers reports that there have been 168,164 farm attacks and 22,786 farm murders since 2010. The Blood Sisters believe 90% of the increases are connected to resentment caused by racial discrimination and unemployment, which is around 50%. Recently, the London Times reported that youth unemployment between the ages of 15 and 24 is at 75%. While 16.3 million people are on social grants, only 3.1 million serve as an income tax base.

All of the farm massacres Southern discovered included what felt like twisted elements resulting from a depraved mind. The drowning of a 12-year-old in boiling hot water, an elderly man ambushed and shot execution style in the head six times in his own home, and an elderly woman strangled and her eyes gouged out with a kitchen fork are just a few of the incidents. Unfortunately, the government offers little assistance, and rural farmers have to coordinate their own protection. One interviewee told Southern that when white South Africans did hold a mass protest against farm murders on Black Monday, the Minister of Defense threatened a civil war if it were ever done again. Though the rise in anti-white violent crime is most potent in rural areas, the situation does not only impact rural farmers. Southern also interviewed a paint ball shop outside of Port Elizabeth that experienced over 100 break-ins, some of which were violent, in a 10-year period, forcing the shop to close down.

Unfortunately, the most charitable reading that can be made of ANC party officials is that they are unconcerned about the plight of white farmers, which is mainly a creation of their own making. Thabo Mokwena, a member of the ANC's provincial executive committee, characterized the policy of the government forcibly taking land from white farmers without compensation as a good objective. Even without forced resettlement, the Black Economic Empowerment Policy has led to the destruction of many farms as utility companies, forced to lay off most of their white workers, are unable to respond to drought conditions. Southern also interviewed lower-class whites living in squatter camps who were denied jobs and healthcare because of the color of their skin. And these conditions exist under the guidance of the ANC, who, compared to other organizations, are the moderates.

Southern interviewed the Deputy President of the Black First Land First organization who told her that because black people's lived experience had not improved since the ending of apartheid, her organization aimed "to put the land and economy back in the hands of black South Africans." It should be noted she said this even as her country's government is overwhelmingly controlled by parties that claim to be affiliated and promoting black interests. Yet this political situation has somehow been unable to "obtain freedom" for the "black majority." Because white people have stolen black people's land, as the story goes, it is up to black South Africans to go to "war at farms" and take "everything" that white people own.

Such ultimatums are so absolute that white South Africans are left without any ability to negotiate. Some have left the country of their birth, but that costs around the equivalent of $300,000. Others, like the Suidlanders, are preparing for the possibility of a civil war along racial lines. One exclusively-white community called Orania is in an attempt to maintain white South African "culture" and "tradition." While they do enjoy an almost nonexistent crime rate, their own currency, and security, they only have a little over 5,000 people. None of these solutions are desirable for most white South African farmers who simply want to work their land and enjoy the fruit of their labors without interference.

As people and organizations in the Unites States wrestle with questions of critical race theory, intersectionality, and all that comes with them, including deconstructing history and considering reparations, I hope they will remember what is happening in South Africa. They are farther down the road of a similar path and it is one leading to the destruction of their country. Not only economically, but also morally. Last summer, as cities burned and rioters threatened to take their path of destruction to the suburbs in order to supposedly fight against racial injustice, no one aware of the situation plaguing South Africa was confused. They had seen it before. They understood the Marxist thinking behind it. As neighborhoods form watch groups, funding is cut for police, and children are short-circuited by a simplified retelling of history to hate their family and country instead of love them, will we learn their lesson?